Perfect Questions Perfect Answers

On an ancient island in Bengal, between the waters of the Ganges and the Sarasvati, a young Peace Corps. worker began a mystical, inner journey into a new and deeper reality...

BOOKS by

His Divine Grace
A.C. Bhaktivedanta Swami Prabhupāda

published by *Krishna Books Inc*

Bhagavad-gītā As It Is
Śrīmad Bhāgavatam (30 volume set)
Śrī Caitanya-caritāmṛta (17 volume set)
Kṛṣṇa, the Supreme Personality of Godhead
Teachings of Lord Chaitanya
Teachings of Queen Kuntī
Śrī Īśopaniṣad
The Nectar of Devotion
The Science of Self-Realization
Rāja-vidyā: The King of Knowledge
Easy Journey to Other Planets
Kṛṣṇa, the Reservoir of Pleasure
The Perfection of Yoga
Beyond Birth and Death
On Chanting Hare Kṛṣṇa
Life Comes From Life
The Path of Perfection
Perfect Questions, Perfect Answers
Search for Liberation

Perfect Questions
Perfect Answers

Conversations Between
His Divine Grace
A.C. Bhaktivedanta
Swami Prabhuāpda
and Bob Cohen,
a Peace Corps worker
in India

Perfect Questions, Perfect Answers

Contains the text and art originally published
by the *Bhaktivedanta Book Trust* in 1977.

Krishna Books Inc is licensed by the
Bhaktivedanta Book Trust
to print and publish the literary works of

His Divine Grace
A. C. Bhaktivedanta Swami Prabhupāda

Readers interested in obtaining other titles by the
author may contact Krishna Books Inc:

www.krishnabooks.org
or email: info@krishnabooks.org

Library of Congress Catalog Card Number: 74-27525
Original ISBN: 0-912776-62-5

KBI Reprint 2015

Printed and bound by Thomson Press (India) Ltd.

Contents

Introduction

God, spiritual life—those were such vague terms to me before I met Śrīla Prabhupāda. I have always been interested in religion, but before I met the Kṛṣṇa conscious devotees, somehow I did not have the proper perspective needed to inquire fruitfully about spiritual life. The existence of a Creator is only common sense—but who is God? Who am I? I had been to Hebrew School and had studied Oriental philosophy, but I could never get satisfying answers to my questions.

I first heard the Hare Kṛṣṇa *mantra* in Greenwich Village, New York, in late 1968.

Hare Kṛṣṇa Hare Kṛṣṇa
Kṛṣṇa Kṛṣṇa Hare Hare
Hare Rāma Hare Rāma
Rāma Rāma Hare Hare

The chanting was captivating, and it made me feel very comfortable. The *mantra* stuck in my mind, and I soon regretted that I had not taken a magazine from the devotees. As explained to me later, a transcendental seed had been planted that could eventually ripen into love of Godhead.

Several months later, I came across a card with the Hare Kṛṣṇa *mantra* on it. The card promised, "Chant these names of God, and your life will be sublime!" I would occasionally chant, and I found that the *mantra* did, in fact, give me a feeling of peace of mind.

After graduating from college with a B.S. in chemistry, I joined the Peace Corps in 1971 and went to India as a science teacher. In India I inquired about the Hare Kṛṣṇa movement. I was attracted by the chanting and intrigued by the philosophy, and I was curious about the movement's authenticity. I had visited the Kṛṣṇa temple in New York several times before going to India, but I did not consider the seemingly austere life of a devotee for myself.

In India I first met the Kṛṣṇa conscious devotees at a festival they were holding in Calcutta during October of 1971. The devotees explained to me the purpose of *yoga* and the need to inquire about spiritual life. I began to feel that the rituals and ceremonies they practiced were not dull, sentimental obligations, but a real, sensible way of life.

At first, however, it was very difficult for me to understand the philosophy of Kṛṣṇa consciousness. In so many subtle ways, my Western upbringing prevented me from seeing things that were as plain as the nose on my face! Fortunately the devotees convinced me of the need to practice some few basic austerities, and in this way I began to gain some insight into spiritual life. I can now recall how distant and tenuous were my concepts of spirituality and transcendental existence. I met Śrīla Prabhupāda briefly at this time—in November of 1971—and shortly thereafter I decided to become a vegetarian. (I was proud of being a vegetarian, but later Śrīla Prabhupāda reminded me that even pigeons are, too.)

In February of 1972, I met some devotees in Calcutta who invited me to a festival in Māyāpur (a holy island ninety miles to the north). The festival was to be held in honor of Lord Caitanya Mahāprabhu, who is considered an incarnation of Kṛṣṇa Himself. I had then been planning a trip to Nepal, but the Peace Corps denied me permission to leave India, and so I went to Māyāpur.

I left for Māyāpur planning to stay for two days at the

most, but I ended up staying a week. I was the only Western nondevotee on the island, and since I was living with the devotees on their land, this was a unique opportunity to learn intimately about Kṛṣṇa consciousness.

On the third day of the festival, I was invited in to see Śrīla Prabhupāda. He was living in a small hut—half-brick and half-thatched, with two or three pieces of simple furniture. Śrīla Prabhupāda asked me to be seated and then asked how I was and whether I had any questions. The devotees had explained to me that Śrīla Prabhupāda could answer my questions because he represents a disciplic succession of spiritual masters. I thought that Śrīla Prabhupāda might really know what is going on in the world. After all, his devotees claimed this, and I admired and respected them. So with this in mind I began to ask my questions. Inadvertently, I had approached a *guru,* or spiritual master, in the prescribed way—by submissively asking questions about spiritual life.

Śrīla Prabhupāda seemed pleased with me, and over the next several days, he answered my questions. I asked them mostly from an academic point of view, but he always gave me personal answers so that I would actually spiritualize my life. His answers were logical, scientific, satisfying and amazingly lucid. Before I met Śrīla Prabhupāda and his disciples, spiritual life was always obscure and nebulous. But the discussions with Śrīla Prabhupāda were realistic, clear and exciting! Śrīla Prabhupāda was patiently trying to help me understand that Kṛṣṇa—God—is the supreme enjoyer, supreme friend and supreme proprietor. I put forward many impediments to accepting the obvious: that I would have to become serious about God consciousness to understand God. But Śrīla Prabhupāda relentlessly yet

kindly urged me on. Even though I had little ability to express myself, Śrīla Prabhupāda understood my every inquiry and answered perfectly.

Bob Cohen
August 14, 1974

ONE

Kṛṣṇa, the All-Attractive February 27, 1972

BOB: What is a scientist?

ŚRĪLA PRABHUPĀDA: One who knows things as they are.

BOB: He thinks he knows things as they are.

ŚRĪLA PRABHUPĀDA: What?

BOB: He hopes he knows things as they are.

ŚRĪLA PRABHUPĀDA: No, he is supposed to know. We approach the scientist because he is supposed to know things correctly. A scientist means one who knows things as they are. Kṛṣṇa means "all-attractive."

BOB: All-attractive.

ŚRĪLA PRABHUPĀDA: Yes. So unless God is all-attractive, how can He be God? A man is important when he is attractive. Is it not?

BOB: It is so.

ŚRĪLA PRABHUPĀDA: So, God must be attractive and attractive for all. Therefore, if God has any name, or if you want to give any name to God, only "Kṛṣṇa" can be given.

BOB: But why only the name Kṛṣṇa?

ŚRĪLA PRABHUPĀDA: Because He's all-attractive. Kṛṣṇa means "all-attractive."

BOB: Oh, I see.

ŚRĪLA PRABHUPĀDA: Yes. God has no name, but by His qualities we give Him names. If a man is very beautiful, we call him "beautiful." If a man is very intelligent, we call him "wise." So the name is given according to the quality. Because God is all-attractive, the name Kṛṣṇa can be applied only to Him. Kṛṣṇa means "all-attractive." It includes everything.

BOB: But what about a name meaning "all-powerful"?

ŚRĪLA PRABHUPĀDA: Yes.... Unless you are powerful, how can you be all-attractive?

ŚYĀMASUNDARA [an American devotee, Śrīla Prabhupāda's secretary]: It includes everything.

ŚRĪLA PRABHUPĀDA: Everything. He must be very beautiful, He must be very wise, He must be very powerful, He must be very famous...

BOB: Is Kṛṣṇa attractive to rascals?

ŚRĪLA PRABHUPĀDA: Oh, yes! He was the greatest rascal also.

BOB: How is that?

ŚRĪLA PRABHUPĀDA: [*laughing*] Because He was always teasing the *gopīs*.

ŚYĀMASUNDARA: Teasing?

ŚRĪLA PRABHUPĀDA: Yes. Sometimes when Rādhārāṇī would go out, Kṛṣṇa would attack Her, and when She would fall down—"Kṛṣṇa, don't torture Me in that way"—They would fall down, and Kṛṣṇa would take the opportunity and kiss Her. [*He laughs.*] So, Rādhārāṇī was very pleased, but superficially Kṛṣṇa was the greatest rascal. So unless rascaldom is in Kṛṣṇa, how could rascaldom be existent in the world? Our formula of God is that He is the source of everything. Unless rascaldom is in Kṛṣṇa, how can it be manifest... because He is the source of everything. But His rascaldom is so nice that everyone worships His rascaldom.

BOB: What about the rascals who are not so nice?

ŚRĪLA PRABHUPĀDA: No, rascaldom is not nice, but Kṛṣṇa is absolute. He is God. Therefore His rascaldom is also good. Kṛṣṇa is all-good. God is good.

BOB: Yes.

ŚRĪLA PRABHUPĀDA: Therefore, when He becomes a rascal, that is also good. That is Kṛṣṇa. Rascaldom is not good, but when it is practiced by Kṛṣṇa, because He is absolutely good, that rascaldom is also good. This one has to understand.

BOB: Are there some people who do not find Kṛṣṇa attractive?

ŚRĪLA PRABHUPĀDA: No. All people will find Him attractive. Who is not attracted? Just give an example: "This man or this living entity is not attracted to Kṛṣṇa." Just find such a person.

BOB: Somebody who wishes to do things in life that he may feel are wrong but who wishes to gain power or prestige or money...

ŚRĪLA PRABHUPĀDA: Yes.

BOB:... may find God unattractive. He may not find God attractive, because God gives him guilt.

ŚRĪLA PRABHUPĀDA: No, not God. His attraction is to become powerful. A man wants to become powerful or rich—is it not? But nobody is richer than Kṛṣṇa. Therefore Kṛṣṇa is attractive to him.

BOB: If a person who wants to become rich prays to Kṛṣṇa, will he become rich?

ŚRĪLA PRABHUPĀDA: Oh, yes!

BOB: He can become rich through this means?

ŚRĪLA PRABHUPĀDA: Oh, yes. Because Kṛṣṇa is all-powerful, if you pray to Kṛṣṇa to become rich, Kṛṣṇa will make you rich.

BOB: If somebody lives an evil life but prays to become rich, he may still become rich?

ŚRĪLA PRABHUPĀDA: Yes. Praying to Kṛṣṇa is not evil.

BOB: Oh, yes.

ŚRĪLA PRABHUPĀDA: [*chuckling*] Somehow or other he prays to Kṛṣṇa, so you cannot say that he is evil.

BOB: Yes.

ŚRĪLA PRABHUPĀDA: Kṛṣṇa says in *Bhagavad-gītā, api cet sudurācāro bhajate mām ananya-bhāk*. Have you read it?

BOB: Yes. The Sanskrit I don't know, but the English I do.

ŚRĪLA PRABHUPĀDA: Hm-m.

BOB: "Even if the most evil man prays to Me..."

ŚRĪLA PRABHUPĀDA: Yes.

BOB: "... He will be elevated."

ŚRĪLA PRABHUPĀDA: Yes. As soon as he begins to pray to Kṛṣṇa, that is not evil. Therefore He is all-attractive. It is said in the *Vedas* that the Absolute Truth, or the Supreme Personality of Godhead, is the reservoir of all pleasure—*raso vai saḥ*. Everyone is hankering after someone because he realizes some mellow in it.

BOB: Excuse me?

ŚRĪLA PRABHUPĀDA: Some mellow. Suppose a man is drinking. Why is he drinking? He is getting some mellow out of that drinking. A man is hankering after money because by possessing money he gets a mellow out of it.

BOB: What does mellow mean?

ŚRĪLA PRABHUPĀDA: [*to Śyāmasundara*] How do they define mellow?

ŚYĀMASUNDARA: Taste, pleasure.

BOB: OK.

ŚRĪLA PRABHUPĀDA: Pleasing taste. So the Vedas say, *raso vai saḥ*. The exact translation of mellow is *rasa*. [*Mālatī, Śyāmasundara's wife, enters with a tray of food*]

What is that?
MĀLATĪ: Eggplant, fried.
ŚRĪLA PRABHUPĀDA: Oh! All-attractive! All-attractive! [*Laughter.*]
ŚYĀMASUNDARA: How is Kṛṣṇa the greatest scientist?
ŚRĪLA PRABHUPĀDA: Because He knows everything. A scientist is one who knows a subject matter thoroughly. He is a scientist. Kṛṣṇa—He knows everything.
BOB: I am presently a science teacher.
ŚRĪLA PRABHUPĀDA: Yes, teaching. But, unless you have perfect knowledge, how can you teach? That is our question.
BOB: Without perfect knowledge, though, you can teach—
ŚRĪLA PRABHUPĀDA: That is cheating; that is not teaching. That is cheating. Just like the scientists say, "There was a chunk... and the creation took place. Perhaps. Maybe..." What is this? Simply cheating! It is not teaching; it is cheating.
BOB: Let me repeat what you said this morning—that was interesting. I asked about miracles, and you said that only a fool would believe in miracles because—let us say you are a child and an adult lifts this table. That's a miracle. Or you're a chemist and you combine acid and base and you make smoke, an explosion or whatever. To somebody ignorant, that's a miracle. But for everything there is a process, and so when you see a miracle, it's just ignorance of the process. So that only a fool would believe in miracles, and—you correct me if I say wrong...
ŚRĪLA PRABHUPĀDA: Yes, yes.
BOB: You said when Jesus came the people then were somewhat more ignorant and needed miracles as aid. I wasn't sure if that's quite what you said.

ŚRĪLA PRABHUPĀDA: Yes, yes. Miracles are for the ignorant.

BOB: I had asked this in relation to all the miracle men you hear about in India.

ŚRĪLA PRABHUPĀDA: Kṛṣṇa is the highest miracle man.

BOB: Yes.

ŚRĪLA PRABHUPĀDA: That is stated by Kuntī...

BOB: Without perfect knowledge, can I not teach some things? For example, I may—

ŚRĪLA PRABHUPĀDA: You can teach up to the point you know.

BOB: Yes, but I should not claim to teach more than I know.

ŚRĪLA PRABHUPĀDA: Yes, that is cheating.

ŚYĀMASUNDARA: In other words, he can't teach the truth with partial knowledge.

ŚRĪLA PRABHUPĀDA: Yes. That is not possible for any human being. A human being has imperfect senses. So how can he teach perfect knowledge? Suppose you see the sun as a disc. You have no means to approach the sun. If you say that we can see the sun by telescope and this and that, they are also made by you, and you are imperfect. So how can your machine be perfect? Therefore, your knowledge of the sun is imperfect. So don't teach about the sun unless you have perfect knowledge. That is cheating.

BOB: But what about to teach that it is supposed that the sun is 93,000,000 miles away?

ŚRĪLA PRABHUPĀDA: As soon as you say "it is supposed," it is not scientific.

BOB: But I think that almost all science, then, is not scientific.

ŚRĪLA PRABHUPĀDA: That is the point!

BOB: All science is based on, you know, suppositions of this or that.

ŚRĪLA PRABHUPĀDA: Yes. They are teaching imperfectly. Just like they are advertising so much about the moon. Do you think their knowledge is perfect?

BOB: No.

ŚRĪLA PRABHUPĀDA: Then?

BOB: What is the proper duty of the teacher in society? Let us say a science teacher. What should he be doing in the classroom?

ŚRĪLA PRABHUPĀDA: Classroom? You should simply teach about Kṛṣṇa.

BOB: He should not teach about...

ŚRĪLA PRABHUPĀDA: No. That will include everything. His aim should be to know Kṛṣṇa.

BOB: Can a scientist teach the science of combining acid and alkaline, and this kind of science, with Kṛṣṇa as its object?

ŚRĪLA PRABHUPĀDA: How can it be?

BOB: If you—when one studies science, one finds general tendencies of nature, and these general tendencies of nature point to a controlling force....

ŚRĪLA PRABHUPĀDA: That I was explaining the other day. I asked one chemist whether, according to chemical formulas, hydrogen and oxygen linked together become water. Do they not?

BOB: It's true.

ŚRĪLA PRABHUPĀDA: Now, there is a vast amount of water in the Atlantic Ocean and Pacific Ocean. What quantity of chemicals was required?

BOB: How much?

ŚRĪLA PRABHUPĀDA: Yes. How many tons?

BOB: Many!
ŚRĪLA PRABHUPĀDA: So who supplied it?
BOB: This was supplied by God.
ŚRĪLA PRABHUPĀDA: Somebody must have supplied it.
BOB: Yes.
ŚRĪLA PRABHUPĀDA: So that is science. You can teach like that.
BOB: Should one bother teaching that if you combine acid and alkaline they form a neutral?
ŚRĪLA PRABHUPĀDA: The same thing. There are so many effervescents. So, who is performing it? Who is supplying the acid and alkaline? [*There is a long pause.*]
BOB: So this comes from the same source as the water.
ŚRĪLA PRABHUPĀDA: Yes. You cannot manufacture water unless you have hydrogen and oxygen. So, here is a vast—not only this Atlantic or Pacific: there are millions of planets, and there are millions of Atlantic and Pacific oceans. So who created this water with hydrogen and oxygen, and how was it supplied? That is our question. Somebody must have supplied it, otherwise how has it come into existence?
BOB: But should it also be taught how you make water from hydrogen and oxygen? The procedure of burning them together—should this also be taught? That is, you burn hydrogen and oxygen together...
ŚRĪLA PRABHUPĀDA: That is secondary. That is not very difficult. Just like Mālatī made this *puri* [a kind of bread]. So, there is flour, and there is *ghee* [clarified butter], and she made a *puri*. But unless there is *ghee* and flour, where is the chance of making a *puri*? In the *Bhagavad-gītā* there is this statement: "Water, earth, air, fire—they are My energies." What is your body? This external body—that is

your energy. Do you know that? Your body is made out of your energy. For example, I am eating...

BOB: Yes.

ŚRĪLA PRABHUPĀDA: So I am creating some energy, and therefore my body is maintained.

BOB: Oh, I see.

ŚRĪLA PRABHUPĀDA: So therefore your body is made out of your energy.

BOB: But when you eat the food, there is energy from the sun in the food.

ŚRĪLA PRABHUPĀDA: So, I am giving an example. I am creating some energy by digesting the food, and that is maintaining my body. If your energy supply is not proper, then your body becomes weak or unhealthy. Your body is made out of your own energy. Similarly, this gigantic cosmic body—the universe—is made of Kṛṣṇa's energy. How can you deny it? As your body is made out of your energy, similarly the universal body must be made by somebody's energy. That is Kṛṣṇa. [*There is a long pause.*]

BOB: I'll have to think about it to follow that.

ŚRĪLA PRABHUPĀDA: What is to follow? It is a fact. [*He laughs.*] Your hair is growing daily. Why? Because you have some energy.

BOB: The energy I obtain from my food.

ŚRĪLA PRABHUPĀDA: Somehow or other you have obtained that energy! And through that energy your hair is growing. So if your body is manufactured by your energy, similarly the whole gigantic manifestation is made of God's energy. It is a fact! It is not *your* energy.

BOB: Yes. Oh, I see that.

A DEVOTEE: Just like—aren't the planets in this universe the sun's energy—a product of the sun's energy?

ŚRĪLA PRABHUPĀDA: Yes, but who produced the sun? That is Kṛṣṇa's energy. Because it is heat, and Kṛṣṇa says, *bhūmir āpo 'nalo vāyuḥ:* "Heat—that is My energy." The sun is the representation of the heating energy of Kṛṣṇa. It is not your energy. You cannot say, "The sun is made by me." But somebody must have made it, and Kṛṣṇa says that He did. So, we believe Kṛṣṇa. Therefore we are Kṛṣṇa-ites.
BOB: Kṛṣṇa-ites?
ŚRĪLA PRABHUPĀDA: Yes. Our knowledge is perfect. If I say that heat is the energy of Kṛṣṇa, you cannot deny it, because it is not your energy. In your body there is some certain amount of heat. Similarly, heat is someone's energy. And who is that person? That is Kṛṣṇa. Kṛṣṇa says, "Yes, it is My energy." So my knowledge is perfect. Because I take the version of the greatest scientist, I am the greatest scientist. I may be a fool personally, but because I take knowledge from the greatest scientist, I am the greatest scientist. I have no difficulty.
BOB: Excuse me?
ŚRĪLA PRABHUPĀDA: I have no difficulty in becoming the greatest scientist because I take the knowledge from the greatest scientist. [*There is a long pause.*] "This earth, water, fire, air, ether, mind, intelligence and ego—they are My eight separated energies."
BOB: They are *separated* energies?
ŚRĪLA PRABHUPĀDA: Yes. Just like this milk. What is this milk? The separated energy of the cow. [*Śyāmasundara and Bob, stunned, laugh in realization.*] Is it not? It is the manifestation of the separated energy of the cow.
ŚYĀMASUNDARA: Is it like a by-product?
ŚRĪLA PRABHUPĀDA: Yes.
BOB: So, what is the significance of this energy's being

separated from Kṛṣṇa?

ŚRĪLA PRABHUPĀDA: "Separated" means that this is made out of the body of the cow but it is not the cow. That is separation.

BOB: So, this earth and all is made out of Kṛṣṇa but it is not Kṛṣṇa?

ŚRĪLA PRABHUPĀDA: It is not Kṛṣṇa. Or, you can say, Kṛṣṇa and not Kṛṣṇa simultaneously. That is our philosophy. One and different. You cannot say that these things are different from Kṛṣṇa, because without Kṛṣṇa they have no existence. At the same time, you cannot say, "Then let me worship water. Why Kṛṣṇa? The pantheists say that because everything is God, whatever we do is God worship. This is Māyāvāda philosophy—that because everything is made of God, therefore everything is God. But our philosophy is that everything is God but also not God.

BOB: So what on earth is God? Is there anything on earth that is God?

ŚRĪLA PRABHUPĀDA: Yes. Because everything is made out of the energy of God. But that does not mean that by worshiping anything you are worshiping God.

BOB: So what is on earth that is not *māyā* [illusion]? It is...

ŚRĪLA PRABHUPĀDA: *Māyā* means "energy."

BOB: It means energy?

ŚRĪLA PRABHUPĀDA: Yes. *Māyā*—and another meaning is "illusion." So foolish persons accept the energy as the energetic. That is *māyā*. Just like sunshine. Sunshine enters your room. Sunshine is the energy of the sun. But because the sunshine enters your room, you cannot say that the sun has entered. If the sun enters your room, then your room and yourself—everything—will be finished. Immediately. You will not have the leisure to understand that the sun has entered. Is it not?

BOB: It is so.

ŚRĪLA PRABHUPĀDA: But you cannot say that sunshine is not the sun. Without the sun, where is the sunshine? So you cannot say that sunshine is not the sun. But at the same time, it is not the sun. It is the sun and not the sun—both. That is our philosophy. *Acintya-bhedābheda*—inconceivable. In the material sense, you cannot conceive that a thing is simultaneously positive and negative. That you cannot think of. That is inconceivable energy. And because everything is Kṛṣṇa's energy, Kṛṣṇa can manifest Himself from any energy. Therefore, when we worship Kṛṣṇa in a form made of something—of earth, water or something like that—that is Kṛṣṇa. You cannot say that it is not Kṛṣṇa. When we worship this metal form of Kṛṣṇa [the Deity form in the temple], that is Kṛṣṇa. That's a fact, because metal is an energy of Kṛṣṇa. Therefore, it is nondifferent from Kṛṣṇa, and Kṛṣṇa is so powerful that He can present Himself fully in His energy. So this Deity worship is not heathenism. It is actually worship of God, provided you know the process.

BOB: If you know the process, then the Deity becomes Kṛṣṇa?

ŚRĪLA PRABHUPĀDA: Not becomes—it *is* Kṛṣṇa.

BOB: The Deity is Kṛṣṇa, but only if you know the process?

ŚRĪLA PRABHUPĀDA: Yes. Just like this electric wire—it is electricity. One who knows the process, he can derive electricity out of it.

ŚYĀMASUNDARA: Otherwise it's just wire.

ŚRĪLA PRABHUPĀDA: Just wire.

BOB: So if I build a statue of Kṛṣṇa, it is not Kṛṣṇa unless...

ŚRĪLA PRABHUPĀDA: It is Kṛṣṇa. But you have to know the process of understanding that it is Kṛṣṇa. It is Kṛṣṇa.
BOB: It is not just earth and mud.
ŚRĪLA PRABHUPĀDA: No. Earth has no separate existence without Kṛṣṇa. Kṛṣṇa says, "My energy." You cannot separate the energy from the energetic. It is not possible. You cannot separate heat from fire. But fire is different from the heat, and heat is different from the fire. You are taking heat; that does not mean you are touching fire. Fire, in spite of emanating heat, keeps its identity. Similarly, although Kṛṣṇa, by His different energies, is creating everything, He remains Kṛṣṇa. The Māyāvādī philosophers think that if Kṛṣṇa is everything, then Kṛṣṇa's separate identity is lost. That is material thinking. For example, by drinking this milk, little by little, when I finish, there is no more milk; it has gone to my belly. Kṛṣṇa is not like that. He is omnipotent. We are utilizing His energy continually; still He is there, present. Just like a man begetting children unlimitedly, but the man is there. A crude example. It's not that because he has produced hundreds of children, he is finished. So, similarly, God or Kṛṣṇa, in spite of His unlimited number of children, is there.

pūrṇasya pūrṇam ādāya
pūrṇam evāvaśiṣyate

"Because He is the complete whole, even though so many complete units emanate from Him, He remains the complete balance." This is Kṛṣṇa consciousness. Kṛṣṇa is never finished. Kṛṣṇa is so powerful. Therefore He is all-attractive. This is one side of the display of Kṛṣṇa's energy. Similarly, He has unlimited energies. This study of Kṛṣṇa's energy is only one side, or a portion only. So in this way, if you go on studying Kṛṣṇa, that is Kṛṣṇa consciousness. It is not a bogus thing—"maybe," "perhaps not." Absolutely! It is!

ŚYĀMASUNDARA: And the study itself is never finished.

ŚRĪLA PRABHUPĀDA: No. How can it be? Kṛṣṇa has unlimited energy.

TWO

Vedic Culture: Varṇāśrama-dharma February 28, 1972

BOB: I've asked devotees about how they feel towards sex in their relations, and I see the way they feel, but I can't see myself acting the same way. See, I'll be getting married at the end of this summer.
ŚRĪLA PRABHUPĀDA: Hm-m?
BOB: I'll be getting married at the end of this summer, in September or August when I return to America. And the devotees say that the householders only have sex to conceive a child, and I cannot picture myself at all in such a position, and—What kind of sex life can one lead, living in the material world?
ŚRĪLA PRABHUPĀDA: The Vedic principle is that one should avoid sex life altogether. The whole Vedic principle is to get liberation from material bondage. There are different attachments for material enjoyment, of which sex life is the topmost enjoyment. The *Bhāgavatam* says that this material world...

puṁsaḥ striyā mithunī-bhāvam etam

Man is attached to woman, and woman is attached to man. Not only in human society—in animal society also. That attachment is the basic principle of material life. So, a woman is hankering or seeking after the association of a man, and a man is hankering or seeking for the association of a woman. All the fiction novels, dramas, cinema and even ordinary advertisements that you see simply depict the attachment between man and woman. Even in the tailor's shop you will find in the window some woman and some man.

pravṛttir eṣā bhūtānāṁ
nivṛttis tu mahāphalām

So this attachment is already there.
BOB: Attachment between man and woman?
ŚRĪLA PRABHUPĀDA: Man and woman. So if you want to get liberation from this material world, then that attachment should be reduced to nil. Otherwise, simply further attachment—You will have to take rebirth, either as a human being or as a demigod or as an animal, as a serpent, as a bird, as a beast. You will have to take birth. So, this basic principle of increasing attachment is not our business, although it is the general tendency. *Gṛha, kṣetra, suta* [home, land, sons]. But if one can reduce and stop it, that is first class. Therefore our Vedic system is to first of all train a boy as a *brahmacārī*—no sex life. The Vedic principle is to reduce attachment, not to increase it. Therefore the whole system is called *varṇāśrama-dharma*. The Indian system calls for *varṇa* and *āśrama*—four social orders and four spiritual orders. *Brahmacarya* [celibate student life], *gṛhastha* [married life], *vānaprastha* [retired life] and *sannyāsa* [renounced life]—these are the spiritual orders. And the social orders consist of *brāhmaṇas* [intellectuals], *kṣatriyas* [administrators], *vaiśyas* [merchants and farmers] and *śūdras* [ordinary workers]. So under this system, the regulative principles are so nice that even if one has the tendency to enjoy material life, he is so nicely molded that at last he achieves liberation and goes back home, back to Godhead. This is the process. So sex life is not required,

but because we are attached to it, therefore there are some regulative principles under which it is maintained. [*chanting starts somewhere in the background, with exotic mṛdaṅga drumbeats amidst laughing and the loud blowing of horns.*]

ŚRĪLA PRABHUPĀDA: It is said in *Śrīmad-Bhāgavatam* that—

puṁsaḥ striyā mithunī-bhāvam etaṁ
tayor mitho hṛdaya-granthim āhuḥ
ato gṛha-kṣetra-sutāpta-vittair
janasya moho 'yam ahaṁ mameti
[Bhāg. 5.5.8]

This sex life is the basic principle of material life—attachment for man or woman. And when they are united, when a man and woman are united, that attachment becomes increased, and that increased attachment will induce one to accumulate *gṛha* (a home), *kṣetra* (land), *suta* (children), *āpta* (friendship or society) and *vitta. Vita* means money. In this way—*gṛha-kṣetra-sutāpta-vittaiḥ*—he becomes entangled. *Janasya moho 'yam:* this is the illusion. And by this illusion he thinks, *ahaṁ mameti:* "I am this body, and anything in relationship with this body is mine."

BOB: What is that again?

ŚRĪLA PRABHUPĀDA: This attachment increases. The material attachment involves thinking, "I am this body, and because I have this body in a particular place, that is my country." And that is going on: "I am American, I am Indian, I am German, I am this, I am that—this body. This is my country. I shall sacrifice everything for my country and society." So in this way, the illusion increases. And under this illusion, when he dies he gets another body.

That may be a superior body or inferior body, according to his *karma*. So if he gets a superior body, then that is also an entanglement, even if he goes to the heavenly planets. But if he becomes a cat or dog, then his life is lost. Or a tree—there is every chance of it. So this science is not known in the world—how the soul is transmigrating from one body to another, and how he is being entrapped in different types of bodies. This science is unknown. Therefore when Arjuna was speaking—"If I kill my brother, if I kill my grandfather on the other side..."—he was simply thinking on the basis of the bodily concept of life. But when his problems could not be solved, he surrendered to Kṛṣṇa and accepted Him as spiritual master. And when Kṛṣṇa became his spiritual master, He chastised Arjuna in the beginning:

aśocyān anvaśocas tvaṁ
prajñā-vādāṁś ca bhāṣase
gatāsūn agatāsūṁś ca
nānuśocanti paṇḍitāḥ

"You are talking like a learned man, but you are fool number one because you are talking about the bodily concept of life." So this sex life increases the bodily concept of life. Therefore, the whole process is to reduce it to nil.

BOB: To reduce it over the stages of your life?

ŚRĪLA PRABHUPĀDA: Yes. Reduce it. A boy is trained as a student up to twenty-five years, restricting sex life. *Brahmacārī*. So, some of the boys remain *naiṣṭhika-brahmacārī* [celibate for life]. Because they are given education and they become fully conversant with spiritual knowledge, they don't want to marry. That is also restricted—he cannot have sex life without being married. Therefore in human society there is marriage, not in animal society.

But people are gradually descending from human society to animal society. They are forgetting marriage. That is also predicted in the *śāstras*. *Dāmpatye 'bhirucir hetuḥ:* in the *Kali-yuga* [the present age of quarrel], eventually there will be no marriage performances; the boy and the girl will simply agree to live together, and their relationship will exist on sexual power. If the man or the woman is deficient in sex life, then there is divorce. So, for this philosophy there are many Western philosophers like Freud and others who have written so many books. But according to Vedic culture, we are interested in sex only for begetting children, that's all. Not to study the psychology of sex life. There is already natural psychology for that. Even if one does not read any philosophy, he is sexually inclined. Nobody is taught it in the schools and colleges. Everyone already knows how to do it. [*He laughs.*] That is the general tendency. But education should be given to *stop it*. That is real education. [*There is a long pause, filled with the sound of bicycle horns, children playing, and throngs of people calling to one another*]

BOB: Presently, in America, that's a radical concept.

ŚRĪLA PRABHUPĀDA: Well, in America there are so many things that require reformation, and this Kṛṣṇa consciousness movement will bring that. I went to your country and saw that the boys and girls were living like friends, so I said to my students, "You cannot live together as friends; you must get yourselves married."

BOB: Many people see that even marriage is not sacred, so they find no desire to marry. Because people get married, and if things are not proper, they get a divorce so very easily—

ŚRĪLA PRABHUPĀDA: Yes, that also.
BOB:—that some people feel that to get married is not meaningful.
ŚRĪLA PRABHUPĀDA: No, their idea is that marriage is for legalized prostitution. They think like that, but that is not marriage. Even that Christian paper—what is that? Watch—?
ŚYĀMASUNDARA: Watchtower?
ŚRĪLA PRABHUPĀDA: Watchtower. It has criticized that one priest has allowed a marriage between two men—homosexuality. So these things are all going on. They take it purely for prostitution, that's all. So therefore people are thinking, "What is the use of keeping a regular prostitute at such heavy expenditure? Better not to have this."
ŚYĀMASUNDARA: You use that example of the cow and the market.
ŚRĪLA PRABHUPĀDA: Yes—when the milk is available in the marketplace, what is the use of keeping a cow? [*Everyone laughs.*] It is a very abominable condition in the Western countries—I have seen it. Here also in India, gradually it is coming. Therefore we have started this Kṛṣṇa consciousness movement to educate people in the essential principles of spiritual life. It is not a sectarian religious movement. It is a cultural movement for everyone's benefit.

THREE

The Real Goal of Life
February 28, 1972 (continued)

ŚRĪLA PRABHUPĀDA: This movement is especially meant to enable a human being to reach the real goal of life.
BOB: The real goal... ?
ŚRĪLA PRABHUPĀDA: The real goal of life.
BOB: Is the real goal of life to know God?
ŚRĪLA PRABHUPĀDA: Yes. To go back home, back to Godhead. That is the real goal of life. The water that comes from the sea forms clouds, the clouds fall down as rain, and the actual goal is to flow down the river and again enter the sea. So, we have come from God, and now we are embarrassed by material life. Therefore, our aim should be to get out of this embarrassing situation and go back home, back to Godhead. This is the real goal of life.

mām upetya punar janma
duḥkhālayam aśāśvatam
nāpnuvanti mahātmānaḥ
saṁsiddhiṁ paramāṁ gatāḥ

["After attaining Me, the great souls, who are *yogīs* in devotion, never return to this temporary world, which is full of miseries, because they have attained the highest perfection."] That is the version of *Bhagavad-gītā*. If anyone comes to Me—*mām upetya:* he does not come back again. Where? To this place—*duḥkhālayam aśāśvatam.* This place is the abode of miseries. Everyone knows, but they have been befooled by so-called leaders. Material life is miserable life. Kṛṣṇa says, God says, that this place is *duḥkhālayam*—it is a place of miseries. And it is also *aśāśvatam*, temporary. You cannot make a compromise: "All right, let it be miserable. I shall remain here as an American or Indian." No. That also you cannot do. You cannot remain an American. You may think that, having been born in America, you are very happy. But you cannot remain an American for long. You will have to be kicked out of that place. And your next life you do not know! Therefore, it is *duḥkhālayam aśāśvatam*—miserable and temporary. That is our philosophy.

BOB: But when you have some knowledge of God, then life is not so miserable?

ŚRĪLA PRABHUPĀDA: No! Some knowledge will not do. You must have perfect knowledge.

janma karma ca me divyam
evaṁ yo vetti tattvataḥ

Tattvataḥ means "perfectly." Perfect knowledge is being taught in *Bhagavad-gītā*. So, we are giving everyone in human society a chance to learn *Bhagavad-gītā* as it is and make his life perfect. That is the Kṛṣṇa consciousness movement. What does your science say about the transmigration of the soul?

BOB: I think... that science... cannot deny or affirm it. Science does not know it.

ŚRĪLA PRABHUPĀDA: Therefore I say that science is imperfect.

BOB: Science may, though, say something. It is said in science that energy is never destroyed; it is changed.

ŚRĪLA PRABHUPĀDA: That's all right. But how the energy is working in the future—that science does not know.

His Divine Grace
A. C. Bhaktivedanta Swami Prabhupāda
Founder-Ācārya
of the Internatinal Society for Krishna Consciousness

'late 1: The world headquarters for the International Society for Krishna
'onsciousness in Mayapur, India.

Plate 2: God is all-attractive, therefore His name is Kṛṣṇa. (*p. 1*)

'late 3: The gigantic cosmic body is made of Kṛṣṇa's energy. (*p. 9*)

Plate 4: God is within the heart of all living beings. (*p. 25*)

'late 5: Everyone is being controlled by the three modes of material ature-goodness, passion and ignorance. (*p.32*)

Plate 6: Kṛṣṇa likes Rādhārāṇi; therefore all the cowherd girls are tryin
to push Her to Kṛṣṇa. (*p. 62*)

How is the energy diverted? How, by different manipulations, is the energy working differently? For instance, electrical energy. By different handling it is operating the heater, and it is operating the refrigerator. They are just the opposite, but the electrical energy is the same. Similarly, this energy—living energy—how is it being directed? Which way is it going? How is it fructifying in the next life? That they do not know. But in *Bhagavad-gītā* it is very simply stated.

vāsāṁsi jīrṇāni yathā vihāya

You are covered by a dress, by a shirt. When this shirt is unusable, you change it. Similarly, this body is just like a shirt and coat. When it is no longer workable, we have to change it.

BOB: What is the "we" that has to change? What is constant?

ŚRĪLA PRABHUPĀDA: That is the soul.

BOB: From one life to the next?

ŚRĪLA PRABHUPĀDA: That is the soul—I. What "you" is speaking? You! What "I" is speaking? Identity: *ātmā*, or soul.

BOB: My soul is different from your soul?

ŚRĪLA PRABHUPĀDA: Yes. You are an individual soul, I am an individual soul.

BOB: You have removed yourself from karmic influences. If I was to remove myself from karmic influences, would our souls be the same or different?

ŚRĪLA PRABHUPĀDA: The soul is of the same quality in all. You are under a certain conception of life at the present moment, and these countrymen of yours [the Kṛṣṇa conscious devotees] were under a certain conception of life, but by training they have taken to another conception of life. So the ultimate training is how to become Kṛṣṇa conscious. That is the perfection.

BOB: If two people are Kṛṣṇa conscious, is their soul the same?

ŚRĪLA PRABHUPĀDA: The soul is always the same.

BOB: In each person? In each person is it the same?

ŚRĪLA PRABHUPĀDA: Yes.

BOB: [*pointing to two devotees*] If these two are Kṛṣṇa conscious, are their souls the same?

ŚRĪLA PRABHUPĀDA: The soul is the same but always individual, even if one is not Kṛṣṇa conscious. For instance, you are a human being, and I am a human being. Even if I am not a Christian, even if you are not a Hindu, still we are human beings. Similarly, the soul may not be Kṛṣṇa conscious, or he may be Kṛṣṇa conscious—it doesn't matter. But the soul is the soul.

BOB: Can you tell me more about this?

ŚRĪLA PRABHUPĀDA: Soul—as pure spirit, all souls are equal. Even in an animal. Therefore it is said, *paṇḍitāḥ sama-darśinaḥ:* those who are actually learned do not see the outward covering, either in a human being or in an animal.

BOB: If I may ask another question on this?

ŚRĪLA PRABHUPĀDA: Yes.

BOB: I have considered the soul somewhat as part of God. At times I think I feel God. I'm here, and you may say God is here. So if the soul is inside me, then should I be able to feel God inside me? Not all of God, I mean, but a...

ŚRĪLA PRABHUPĀDA: Part of God.

BOB: But I don't feel God in me, but God may be here, separate—separate from me. But should I be able to feel

God inside me, since my soul is part of God?

ŚRĪLA PRABHUPĀDA: Yes. God is inside also. God is everywhere. God is inside and outside also. This is to be known.

BOB: How do you feel God inside you?

ŚRĪLA PRABHUPĀDA: Not in the beginning, but you have to know from the *śāstras* [scriptures], by the Vedic information. For example, in the *Bhagavad-gītā* it is said, *īśvaraḥ sarva-bhūtānāṁ hṛd-deśe 'rjuna tiṣṭhati:* God is there in everyone's heart. *Paramāṇu-cayāntara-stham:* God is also within every atom. So this is the first information. And then, by the yogic process, you have to realize it.

BOB: Yogic process?

ŚRĪLA PRABHUPĀDA: Yes.

BOB: Is chanting Hare Kṛṣṇa such a yogic process?

ŚRĪLA PRABHUPĀDA: Yes, it is also a yogic process.

BOB: What kind of yogic process must I do to find out—to feel this information—to feel the soul inside?

ŚRĪLA PRABHUPĀDA: Yes, there are many different yogic processes, but for this age this process is very nice.

BOB: Chanting.

ŚRĪLA PRABHUPĀDA: Yes.

BOB: Through this I can feel not only God outside but God inside?

ŚRĪLA PRABHUPĀDA: You'll understand everything of God—how God is inside, how God is outside, how God is working. Everything will be revealed. By this attitude of service, God will reveal Himself. You cannot understand God by your endeavor. Only if God reveals Himself. For instance, when the sun is out of your sight at night, you cannot see it by your torchlight, or any light. But in the morning you can see the sun automatically, without any torchlight. Similarly, you have to create a situation—you have to put yourself in a situation—in which God will be revealed. It is not that by some method you can ask God, "Please come. I will see You." No, God is not your order carrier.

BOB: You must please God for Him to reveal Himself. Is that correct?

ŚRĪLA PRABHUPĀDA: Yes.

ŚYĀMASUNDARA: How do we know when we are pleasing God?

ŚRĪLA PRABHUPĀDA: When we see Him. Then you will understand. Just as, when you eat, you do not require to ask anyone whether you are feeling strength or your hunger is satisfied. If you eat, you understand that you are feeling energy. You don't need to inquire from anyone. Similarly, if you actually serve God, then you will understand, "God is dictating to me. God is there. I am seeing God."

A DEVOTEE: Or God's representative.

ŚRĪLA PRABHUPĀDA: Yes.

DEVOTEE: It comes easier.

ŚRĪLA PRABHUPĀDA: You have to go through God's representative.

yasya prasādād bhagavat-prasādaḥ

"By the mercy of the spiritual master one is benedicted by the mercy of Kṛṣṇa." If you please God's representative, then automatically God becomes pleased, and thus you can directly see Him.

AN INDIAN GENTLEMAN: How to please God's representative?

ŚRĪLA PRABHUPĀDA: You have to carry out his orders,

that's all. God's representative is the *guru*. He asks you to do this, to do that—if you do that, that is pleasing.

yasyāprasādān na gatiḥ kuto 'pi

"Without the grace of the spiritual master one cannot make any advancement." If you displease him, then you are nowhere. Therefore we worship the *guru*.

sākṣād-dharitvena samasta-śāstrair
uktas tathā bhāvyata eva sadbhiḥ
kintu prabhor yaḥ priya eva tasya
vande guroḥ śrī-caraṇāravindam

["The spiritual master is to be honored as much as the Supreme Lord because of his being the most confidential servitor of the Lord. This is acknowledged by all revealed scriptures and is followed by all authorities. Therefore I offer my respectful obeisances unto the lotus feet of such a spiritual master, who is a bona fide representative of Lord Kṛṣṇa."] The *guru* should be accepted as God. That is the injunction of all *śāstra*.

BOB: The *guru* should be accepted as a representative of God?

ŚRĪLA PRABHUPĀDA: Yes, the *guru* is God's representative. The *guru* is the external manifestation of Kṛṣṇa.

BOB: But different from the incarnations of Kṛṣṇa that come?

ŚRĪLA PRABHUPĀDA: Yes.

BOB: In what way is the external manifestation of the *guru* different from the external manifestation of, let us say, Kṛṣṇa or Caitanya when They come to earth?

ŚRĪLA PRABHUPĀDA: The *guru* is the representative of Kṛṣṇa. So there are symptoms of who is a *guru*. The general symptoms are described in the *Vedas*.

tad-vijñānārthaṁ sa gurum evābhigacchet
samit-pāṇiḥ śrotriyaṁ brahma-niṣṭham

A *guru* must come in a disciplic succession, and he must have heard thoroughly about the *Vedas* from his spiritual master. Generally a *guru's* symptom is that he is a perfect devotee, that's all. And he serves Kṛṣṇa by preaching His message.

BOB: Lord Caitanya—He was a different type of *guru* than you are?

ŚRĪLA PRABHUPĀDA: No, no. *Gurus* cannot be of different types. All *gurus* are of one type.

BOB: But He was—was He also an incarnation at the same time?

ŚRĪLA PRABHUPĀDA: Yes, He is Kṛṣṇa Himself, but He is representing the *guru*.

BOB: I... I see.

ŚRĪLA PRABHUPĀDA: Yes.

BOB: And then...

ŚRĪLA PRABHUPĀDA: Because Kṛṣṇa was God, He demanded:

sarva-dharmān parityajya
mām ekaṁ śaraṇaṁ vraja

"Abandon all varieties of religion and just surrender unto Me." But people misunderstood Him. Therefore Kṛṣṇa again came as a *guru* and taught people *how* to surrender to Kṛṣṇa.

ŚYĀMASUNDARA: Doesn't He say in *Bhagavad-gītā*, "I am the spiritual master"?

ŚRĪLA PRABHUPĀDA: Yes, He is the original spiritual

master because He was accepted as spiritual master by Arjuna. So what is the difficulty? *Śiṣyas te 'haṁ śādhi māṁ tvāṁ prapannam.* Arjuna told the Lord, "I am Your disciple, and a soul surrendered unto You. Please instruct me." So unless He is a spiritual master, how does Arjuna become His disciple? He is the original *guru. Tene brahma hṛdā ya ādi-kavaye:* "It is He only who first imparted Vedic knowledge unto the heart of Brahmā, the first created being." Therefore He is the original *guru.*

BOB: Kṛṣṇa.

ŚRĪLA PRABHUPĀDA: Yes. He is the original *guru.* Then His disciple Brahmā is a *guru,* then his disciple Nārada is a *guru,* then his disciple Vyāsa is a *guru*—in this way there is a *guru-paramparā* [disciplic succession of *gurus*]. *Evaṁ paramparā-prāptam:* the transcendental knowledge is received through the disciplic succession.

BOB: So a *guru* receives his knowledge through the disciplic succession, not directly from Kṛṣṇa? Do you receive some knowledge directly from Kṛṣṇa?

ŚRĪLA PRABHUPĀDA: Yes. Kṛṣṇa's direct instruction is there: *Bhagavad-gītā.*

BOB: I see, but...

ŚRĪLA PRABHUPĀDA: But you have to learn it through the disciplic succession, otherwise you will misunderstand it.

BOB: But presently you do not receive information directly from Kṛṣṇa? It comes through the disciplic succession from the books?

ŚRĪLA PRABHUPĀDA: There is no difference. Suppose I say that this is a pencil. If you say to him, "There is a pencil," and if he says to another man, "This is a pencil," then what is the difference between his instruction and my instructions?

BOB: Kṛṣṇa's mercy allows you to know this now?

ŚRĪLA PRABHUPĀDA: You can take Kṛṣṇa's mercy also, provided it is delivered as it is. Just as we are teaching *Bhagavad-gītā*. In *Bhagavad-gītā* Kṛṣṇa says:

sarva-dharmān parityajya
mām ekaṁ śaraṇaṁ vraja

"Just give up all other forms of religion and simply surrender unto Me." Now we are saying that you should give up everything and surrender to Kṛṣṇa. Therefore, there is no difference between Kṛṣṇa's instruction and our instruction. There is no deviation. So if you receive knowledge in that perfect way, that is as good as receiving instruction directly from Kṛṣṇa. But we don't change anything.

BOB: When I pray reverently, faithfully, does Kṛṣṇa hear me?

ŚRĪLA PRABHUPĀDA: Yes.

BOB: From me to Him?

ŚRĪLA PRABHUPĀDA: Yes, because He is within your heat He is always hearing you—whether you are praying or not praying. When you are doing some nonsense, He is also hearing you. And when you pray, that is very good—welcome.

BOB: To Kṛṣṇa's ear, is praying louder than nonsense?

ŚRĪLA PRABHUPĀDA: No. He is all-perfect. He can hear everything. Even if you don't speak, even if you simply think, "I shall do it," then He hears you. *Sarvasya cāhaṁ hṛdi sanniviṣṭaḥ:* Kṛṣṇa is seated in everyone's heart.

BOB: But one should pray—is that so?

ŚRĪLA PRABHUPĀDA: That is his business—praying.

BOB: Whose business?

ŚRĪLA PRABHUPĀDA: Every living entity's. That is the only business. *Eko bahūnāṁ yo vidadhāti kāmān.* That is the statement of the *Vedas.*

BOB: What does that mean?

ŚRĪLA PRABHUPĀDA: He supplies everything to everyone. He is supplying food to everyone. So He is the Father. So why should you not pray, "Father, give me this"? Just as in the Christian Bible there is, "Father, give us our daily bread." That is good—they are accepting the Supreme Father. But grown-up children should not ask from the father; rather, they should be prepared to serve the father. That is *bhakti* [devotion].

BOB: My questions you solve so nicely. [*Everyone laughs with affection.*]

ŚRĪLA PRABHUPĀDA: Thank you very much.

BOB: So, should I ask you another question now?

ŚRĪLA PRABHUPĀDA: Oh, yes. Yes!

FOUR

The Three Modes of Nature February 28, 1972 (continued)

BOB: I have read that there are three *guṇas*—passion, ignorance and goodness—in life. I was wishing that you would explain this somewhat, especially what is meant by the mode of ignorance and the mode of goodness.

ŚRĪLA PRABHUPĀDA: In goodness you can understand things—knowledge. You can know that there is God, that this world was created by Him, and so many things, actual things—the sun is this, the moon is this—perfect knowledge. If one has some knowledge, even though it may not be perfect, that is goodness. And in passion one identifies with his material body and tries to gratify his senses. That is passion. And ignorance is animal life—in ignorance, one does not know what is God, how to become happy, why we are in this world. For example, if you take an animal to the slaughterhouse, it will go. This is ignorance. But a man will protest. If a goat is to be killed after five minutes but you give it a morsel of grass, it is happy because it is eating. Just like a child—even if you are planning to kill her or kill him, he is happy and laughs because he is innocent. That is ignorance.

BOB: Being in these modes determines your *karma*. Is that correct?

ŚRĪLA PRABHUPĀDA: Yes. According to the association of the modes of nature, your activities are being contaminated.

kāraṇaṁ guṇa-saṅgo 'sya
sad-asad-yoni-janmasu

A man gets a higher birth or lower birth according to the association of the *guṇas*, or the modes of nature.

BOB: So cheating and like that—what mode is that?

ŚRĪLA PRABHUPĀDA: Cheating is mixed passion and ignorance. Suppose one man cheats another. That means he wants to obtain something; he is passionate. But if he commits murder, he does not know that he will have to suffer for it, so it is a mixture of passion and ignorance.

BOB: And what about when somebody helps another person?

ŚRĪLA PRABHUPĀDA: That is goodness.

BOB: Why is that goodness? What intelligence is that? I mean—this represents knowledge of what? You said that goodness is when you have knowledge.

ŚRĪLA PRABHUPĀDA: Yes.

BOB: Intelligence.

ŚRĪLA PRABHUPĀDA: Yes.

BOB: So helping another person?

ŚRĪLA PRABHUPĀDA: That means that he is ignorant and you are trying to enlighten him.

BOB: So giving intelligence...

ŚRĪLA PRABHUPĀDA: Yes, that is goodness.

BOB: And what about just giving assistance?

ŚRĪLA PRABHUPĀDA: That is also goodness.

BOB: If a beggar has nothing and you give him alms...

ŚRĪLA PRABHUPĀDA: So that may still be goodness. But in your Bowery Street, they give some charity, and immediately he purchases one bottle of wine and drinks and lies down flat. [*All laugh.*] So that is charity. But that is not goodness; that is ignorance.

BOB: Charity is ignorance?
ŚRĪLA PRABHUPĀDA: There are three kinds of charities—good, passionate and ignorant. Goodness is giving charity where charity must be given. Just like this Kṛṣṇa consciousness movement—if anyone gives charity to this movement, that is goodness because it is spreading God consciousness, Kṛṣṇa consciousness. That is goodness. And if one gives charity for some return, that is passion. And if somebody gives in charity in an improper place and time, without respect and to an unworthy person, just like the Bowery man, that is ignorance. But Kṛṣṇa says:

yat karoṣi yad aśnāsi
yaj juhoṣi dadāsi yat

"All that you do, all that you eat, all that you offer and give away, as well as all austerities that you may perform, should be done as an offering unto Me." If Kṛṣṇa takes, that is the perfection of charity. Or anyone who is a representative of Kṛṣṇa—if he takes, that is perfection.
BOB: And what kind of charity is it when you give food to somebody who is hungry?
ŚRĪLA PRABHUPĀDA: Well, that depends on the circumstances. For example, a doctor has forbidden his patient to take any solid food, and if the patient is asking, "Give me some solids," and if you give him solid food in charity, then you are not doing good to him. That is ignorance.
BOB: Are the devotees beyond accumulating *karma?* These devotees—do they feel *karma?* Do they work in these modes? Are they in the mode of goodness?
ŚRĪLA PRABHUPĀDA: They are above goodness! *Śuddha-sattva.* The devotees are not in this material world. They are in the spiritual world. That is stated in the

Bhagavad-gītā:

māṁ ca yo 'vyabhicāreṇa
bhakti-yogena sevate
sa guṇān samatītyaitān
brahma-bhūyāya kalpate

["One who engages in full devotional service, who does not fall down in any circumstances, at once transcends the modes of material nature and thus comes to the level of Brahman."] Devotees are neither in goodness, passion nor ignorance. They are transcendental to all these qualities.

BOB: A devotee who is very faithful reaches this stage?

ŚRĪLA PRABHUPĀDA: Yes. Devotee... You can become a devotee as they have become. It is not difficult. Simply you have to engage yourself in the transcendental loving service of the Lord, that's all.

BOB: I wish to gain more knowledge of God and be able to feel God's presence more. The reason for this is because I feel life has little meaning without this.

ŚRĪLA PRABHUPĀDA: Yes! If you miss this human form of life, then it is a great loss. That is a great chance given to the living entity to get out of the entanglement of material existence.

BOB: I feel thankful that I've been able to ask these questions...

ŚRĪLA PRABHUPĀDA: Yes, you can learn more and more.

BOB: But I still have... my connections at home. Marriage is... I am engaged....

ŚRĪLA PRABHUPĀDA: No, no. There are so many marriages. [*He indicates Śyāmasundara.*] He is married. Marriage is no barrier. I told you that there are four different orders of spiritual life—*brahmacārī, gṛhastha, vānaprastha* and *sannyāsa*. So after *brahmacārī* life, one can marry. That is not obligatory. One may remain *naiṣṭhika-brahmacārī* for his whole life. But a *brahmacārī* can marry. And after marriage, there is *vānaprastha* life. This means that one is a little aloof from family—the husband and wife live separately. At that time there is no sex life. Then when he is fully renounced, detached from family life, he takes *sannyāsa*.

BOB: Does somebody forget his wife completely then?

ŚRĪLA PRABHUPĀDA: Yes. Forgetting is not very difficult, if you try to forget. Out of sight, out of mind. [*All laugh.*] Just as I have my wife, children, grandchildren—everything. But, out of sight, out of mind, that's all. Therefore, *vānaprastha, sannyāsa*—everything is nicely arranged by the Vedic system.

FIVE

Becoming Pure
February 29, 1972

BOB: Thank you so much for allowing me to ask my questions.

ŚRĪLA PRABHUPĀDA: That is my mission. People should understand the science of God. Unless we cooperate with the Supreme Lord, our life is baffled. I have given the example many times that a screw which has fallen from a machine has no value. But when the same screw is again attached to the machine, it has value. Similarly, we are part and parcel of God. So without God, what is our value? No value! We should again come back to our position of attachment to God. Then we have value.

BOB: I met a fellow today who came in the afternoon. His reason for coming—you may find it humorous—was that he heard the hippies were in Māyāpur.

ŚRĪLA PRABHUPĀDA: What?

BOB: He heard that hippies were in Māyāpur. I was talking to him, and then some devotees were talking to him. He had said some things to me which I could find no answer for. And he said he would come back tomorrow and meet some devotees. But let me tell you what he said. This is confusing. When he was young—

ŚRĪLA PRABHUPĀDA: He's Indian?

BOB: Yes, Indian. He lives nearby and speaks English fairly well. When he was young he worshiped Kālī [a popular demigoddess] every day very rigorously, and then the floods came. When the floods came, the people saw hardship, and now he has no religion, and he says he finds his happiness in trying to develop love among people. And I couldn't think of what to say to him to add God and religion to his life. He says that after he dies, "maybe I'll become part of God, maybe not," but he can't worry about it now. He says he's tried these religious experiences, but they didn't work. One reason I ask this is because when I go back to America, a lot of people I come across are like this. They see that religion, like his worship of Kālī or other kinds of religion they've experienced, doesn't work. And I don't know what to say to them to convince them it's worth trying.

ŚRĪLA PRABHUPĀDA: Do not try at the present moment. You try to be convinced yourself.

BOB: Yes. I asked him to see devotees, but then on the way out, as he was leaving down the road, I met him again and told him, "Come back," but... Oh, I see.

ŚRĪLA PRABHUPĀDA: *You* first of all be convinced. And then try to convince others. Caitanya Mahāprabhu's instruction is that you can improve the welfare of others when your own life is a success:

bhārata-bhūmite haila manuṣya-janma yāra
janma sārthaka kari' kara para-upakāra

First make your life perfect. Then try to teach others.

BOB: The devotees have told me that without consciousness of Kṛṣṇa all the time, you cannot be happy. But at times I feel happy.

ŚRĪLA PRABHUPĀDA: At times. Not always.

BOB: Yes.

ŚRĪLA PRABHUPĀDA: But if you become Kṛṣṇa conscious, you will feel happy always.

BOB: They had implied that you cannot feel happy without Kṛṣṇa consciousness.

ŚRĪLA PRABHUPĀDA: That is a fact. For example, if you are an animal of the land and you are thrown into the water, you cannot be happy in water in any condition. When you are again taken up to the land, then you'll be happy. Similarly, we are part and parcel of Kṛṣṇa. We cannot be happy without being part and parcel of Kṛṣṇa. The same example: the machine part, without the machine, has no value, but when it is again put into the machine it has value. We are part of Kṛṣṇa; we must join Kṛṣṇa. And you can join Kṛṣṇa immediately by your consciousness, simply by thinking, "I am Kṛṣṇa's, Kṛṣṇa is mine." That's all.

BOB: What is that? Kṛṣṇa is...

ŚRĪLA PRABHUPĀDA: Kṛṣṇa is mine.

BOB: Mine?

ŚRĪLA PRABHUPĀDA: Yes. Mine. My Kṛṣṇa.

BOB: Ah.

ŚRĪLA PRABHUPĀDA: Kṛṣṇa is mine. Kṛṣṇa is mine.

BOB: Yes.

ŚRĪLA PRABHUPĀDA: And I am Kṛṣṇa's. That is our actual position.

BOB: We are part of Kṛṣṇa.

ŚRĪLA PRABHUPĀDA: Yes. Everything is part and parcel of Kṛṣṇa. Because everything is generated by the energy of Kṛṣṇa and everything *is* the energy of Kṛṣṇa.

AN INDIAN GENTLEMAN: Śrīla Prabhupāda, I have one question. What is the status of service minus devotion?

ŚRĪLA PRABHUPĀDA: Hm-m? That is not service, that is business. [*Everyone laughs.*] For example, here in Māyāpur we have employed a contractor. That is not service—that is business. Is it not? Sometimes they will advertise, "Our customers are our masters." Is it not? But in spite of the flowery language—"Our customers are our masters"—this is business, because nobody is a qualified customer unless he pays. But service is not like that. Service—Caitanya Mahāprabhu prays to Kṛṣṇa:

yathā tathā vā vidadhātu lampaṭo
mat-prāṇa-nāthas tu sa eva nāparaḥ

"You do whatever You like, but still You are my worshipable Lord." That is service. "I don't ask any return from You." That is service. When you expect some return, that is business.

BOB: I wish to ask you to advise me on how I can come to feel closer to God. I'll be leaving you soon. And I'm—

ŚRĪLA PRABHUPĀDA: You have to be purified.

BOB: I come to the temple at times, and then I leave, and I'm not sure how much I take with me.

ŚRĪLA PRABHUPĀDA: It does not take much time. Within six months you will realize your progress. But you have to follow the regulative principles. Then it will be all right. Just like these boys and girls are doing.

BOB: Yes, I see.

ŚRĪLA PRABHUPĀDA: They have no tendency for going to the cinema or going to a hotel. No. They have stopped all *anarthas,* all unnecessary things.

BOB: I—I feel that when I go back, they'll—

ŚRĪLA PRABHUPĀDA: The whole human life is meant for purification.

BOB: Yes.

ŚRĪLA PRABHUPĀDA:

tapo divyaṁ putrakā yena sattvaṁ
śuddhyed yasmād brahma-saukhyaṁ tv anantam

Sattva means existence. So if you don't purify your existence, then you will have to change your body. From this body to that. Sometimes it may be higher, sometimes lower. For example, if you don't cure a disease, it can put you into trouble in so many ways. Similarly, if you don't purify your existence, then you will have to transmigrate from one body to another. There are very subtle laws of nature. Now there is no guarantee that you will get a very comfortable body or an American body. Therefore, it is essential for the human being to purify his existence. Unless you purify your existence, you will hanker after happiness but will not always be happy.

BOB: When I go to my job in New York, I hope I'll become pure, but I'm sure that I won't become as pure as your devotees here. I—I don't see myself doing that.

ŚRĪLA PRABHUPĀDA: You can do as they are doing. They were not pure in the beginning; now they are pure. Similarly, you can become pure. For example, in your childhood you were not educated—but now you are educated.

BOB: So, what are the things that I may do? When I go back, I must—

ŚRĪLA PRABHUPĀDA: When do you go back?

BOB: I'll be going back to Chaibasa to do my work there, and...

ŚRĪLA PRABHUPĀDA: What is there in Chaibasa?

BOB: That is where I do my teaching. I live there.

ŚRĪLA PRABHUPĀDA: So better not to teach—because you do not know what to teach.

BOB: [*Laughs.*] I'll be going—I don't like this teaching so much, and I'll be returning to America in May, but while I'm here, this is my agreement for staying in India.

ŚRĪLA PRABHUPĀDA: If you are serious, you can keep

yourself pure anywhere. It doesn't matter whether you stay in America or India. But you must know how to keep yourself purified. That's all.

BOB: You mean by following these principles?

ŚRĪLA PRABHUPĀDA: Yes. I went to America, for instance, but either in America or India, I am the same man.

BOB: I—I have tried somewhat to follow since I met you the first time [a brief visit in Calcutta during November, 1971].

ŚRĪLA PRABHUPĀDA: Hm-m. But follow—you must *strictly* follow if you are serious.

BOB: Maybe—OK, maybe—what I say now is—well—the most foolish of all I have said. But let me tell you how I feel.

ŚRĪLA PRABHUPĀDA: No, no, not foolish. I don't say foolish—but imperfect.

BOB: OK. [*He laughs.*] Imperfect. But let me tell you. I feel that right now I admire and respect your devotees, but I don't feel as if I am part of them, or even that I have a great desire to be part of them. I feel that I just want—I want to do what is right, come closer to God, and if—and if I just go to a better life next time—I'd be satisfied.

ŚRĪLA PRABHUPĀDA: Very good.

BOB: I guess it's material clinging, but...

ŚRĪLA PRABHUPĀDA: So, you just follow in their footsteps, and your desire will be fulfilled. We are training them how to become purified and happy. That is our mission. We want to see everyone happy. *Sarve sukhino bhavantu.* People do not know how to become happy. They do not take the standard path to become happy. They manufacture their own way. That is the difficulty. Therefore, Ṛṣabhadeva gave this advice to his sons: "My dear boys, just undergo austerity for transcendental realization." Everyone is performing austerity. This boy I know—he had to go to a foreign country to learn commercial management. Now he is well situated. In this way, everyone must undergo some austerity for future life. So why not take that austerity for *permanent* happiness? You have to purify your existence and your body. As many times as you accept a material body, you will have to change it. But as soon as you get a spiritual body, there is no question of change. You already have a spiritual body. Now, due to our material contamination, we are developing the material body. But if we associate with spiritual life, then we shall develop a spiritual body. The same example I have several times given is that if you put an iron rod within fire, it will become like fire. Is it not?

BOB: Put the iron rod into fire?

ŚRĪLA PRABHUPĀDA: Yes, and it will become like fire.

BOB: Yes.

ŚRĪLA PRABHUPĀDA: Although iron.

BOB: Yes.

ŚRĪLA PRABHUPĀDA: Similarly, if you always keep yourself spiritually engaged, your body will act spiritually, although it is material. The same example: when an iron rod is red-hot, touch it anywhere, and it will burn. It takes on the quality of fire. Similarly, if you always keep yourself in Kṛṣṇa consciousness, then you will become spiritualized. You will act spiritually. No more material demands.

BOB: How do I do this?

ŚRĪLA PRABHUPĀDA: This process. They are doing it. You have seen these boys, our six boys who have been initiated today. It is very simple. You have to follow the four restrictive regulations and chant these beads. Very easy.

BOB: Well, but, see—when I am back in Bihar and following my lifestyle there, I—if I follow all these regulative principles—some I follow now, but not all—

ŚRĪLA PRABHUPĀDA: "Some" means... ?

BOB: "Some"?

ŚRĪLA PRABHUPĀDA: There are only four regulative principles. "Some" means three, or two?

BOB: Two or three.

ŚRĪLA PRABHUPĀDA: So why not the other one?

BOB: No, no. I mean I follow one or two. One or two I follow now.

ŚRĪLA PRABHUPĀDA: [*Laughs.*] Why not the other three? What is the difficulty? Which one do you follow?

BOB: Which one do I follow? Well, I'm almost vegetarian, but I eat eggs.

ŚRĪLA PRABHUPĀDA: Then that is also not complete.

BOB: No, not even complete. Since last time [November], I've become vegetarian, but...

ŚRĪLA PRABHUPĀDA: Vegetarian is no qualification.

BOB: Not much.

ŚRĪLA PRABHUPĀDA: The pigeon is vegetarian. The monkey is vegetarian—the most rubbish creature...

BOB: Well...

ŚRĪLA PRABHUPĀDA: The monkey is vegetarian. This naked *sannyāsī* lives in the forest... the most mischievous...

BOB: I—I felt that it was a little bit of progress because it was somewhat difficult at first, then easy, and I had returned to—

ŚRĪLA PRABHUPĀDA: No, you can stick to all the regulative principles, provided you take to the Kṛṣṇa consciousness process—otherwise it is not possible.

BOB: Yes, this is it. I have—when I'm back in Bihar,

and—um—my friends may say... We're sitting in the evening, and there's nothing to do but fight mosquitoes, and they say, "How about smoking some marijuana?" And I say, "Sure, there's nothing else to do," and then I sit down, and I enjoy myself for the evening. Now we did this, we got carried away, we were doing it every day and realizing we were hurting ourselves and stopped, but still on occasion we...

ŚRĪLA PRABHUPĀDA: You have to live with *us*. Then your friends will not ask you, "What about marijuana?" [*Bob laughs.*] Keep the association of devotees. We are opening centers to give people a chance to associate with us. Why have we taken so much land [in Māyāpur]? Those who are seriously desirous—they will come and live with us. Association is very influential. If you associate with drunkards, you become drunk; if you associate with *sādhus,* then you become a *sādhu.*

ŚYĀMASUNDARA [Śrīla Prabhupāda's secretary]: He can come and stay with you in Bombay.

ŚRĪLA PRABHUPĀDA: Yes, you can stay with us in Bombay. But he wants friends with marijuana. That is the difficulty.

BOB: Let me ask you about something else; then maybe I'll come back to this. I find that I think of myself too much, and this way I can't think of God so much. I think of myself in too many places. How can I forget about myself so I can concentrate on other, more important things?

ŚRĪLA PRABHUPĀDA: As they [the devotees] have done.

BOB: [*Laughs.*] You are saying to me that my path—I think what you're saying is that my path to purity is to become a devotee.

ŚRĪLA PRABHUPĀDA: Do you hesitate?

BOB: Well, I...

ŚRĪLA PRABHUPĀDA: Is it very difficult to become a devotee?

BOB: For myself—it is. I—I don't feel so much the desire. First the devotees tell me that they have given up material life. These four regulative principles, they have explained to me, mean giving up material life, and that I see. And in place of this they have...

ŚRĪLA PRABHUPĀDA: What do you mean by material life? [*Bob is silent*] I am sitting on this bed. Is it material or spiritual?

BOB: Material.

ŚRĪLA PRABHUPĀDA: Then how have we given up material life?

BOB: I think how I interpreted it was "a desire for our material gains..."

ŚRĪLA PRABHUPĀDA: What is material?

BOB: Working towards material gains and not giving up all materials.

ŚRĪLA PRABHUPĀDA: Material life means—when you desire to gratify your senses, that is material life. And when you desire to serve God, that is spiritual life. That is the difference between material life and spiritual life. Now we are trying to serve our senses. But instead of serving the senses, when we serve God, that is spiritual life. What is the difference between our activities and others' activities? We are using everything—table, chair, bed, tape recorder, typewriter—so what is the difference? The difference is that we are using everything for Kṛṣṇa.

BOB: The devotees have said that the sensual pleasures they have given up are replaced with spiritual kinds of pleasures, but—see—I haven't felt this.

ŚRĪLA PRABHUPĀDA: Spiritual pleasures come when you desire to please Kṛṣṇa. That is spiritual pleasure. For example, a mother is more pleased by feeding her son. She's not eating, but when she sees that her son is eating very nicely, then she becomes pleased.

BOB: Hmm-m. Spiritual pleasure, then, is pleasing God.

ŚRĪLA PRABHUPĀDA: Spiritual pleasure means the pleasure of Kṛṣṇa.

BOB: Pleasing Kṛṣṇa.

ŚRĪLA PRABHUPĀDA: Yes. Material pleasure means the pleasure of the senses. That's all. This is the difference. When you simply try to please Kṛṣṇa, that is spiritual pleasure.

BOB: I had viewed this as—my thought of pleasing God was to—

ŚRĪLA PRABHUPĀDA: Don't manufacture your ways of pleasing God. Don't manufacture. Suppose I want to please you. Then I shall ask you, "How can I serve you?" Not that I manufacture some service. That is not pleasing. Suppose I want a glass of water. If you concoct the idea, "Swāmījī will be more pleased if I give him a glass of milk, hot milk," that will not please me. If you want to please me, then you should ask me, "How can I please you?" And if you do what I order, that will please me.

BOB: And pleasing Kṛṣṇa, then, is being a devotee of Kṛṣṇa.

ŚRĪLA PRABHUPĀDA: A devotee is one who is always pleasing Kṛṣṇa. He has no other business. That is a devotee.

BOB: Can you tell me some more about chanting Hare Kṛṣṇa? I have for quite some time chanted, but never regularly—just a little bit here and there. I just got beads very recently, and once in a while I feel comfortable chanting, and once in a while not comfortable at all. Maybe I don't chant properly. I don't know.

ŚRĪLA PRABHUPĀDA: Yes, everything has a process. You have to adopt the process.

BOB: The devotees tell me of the ecstasy they feel when chanting.

ŚRĪLA PRABHUPĀDA: Yes, the more you become purified, the more you will feel ecstasy. This chanting process is the purifying process.

SIX

The Perfect Devotee
February 29, 1972, evening

ŚYĀMASUNDARA: Śrīla Prabhupāda, this afternoon we were discussing austerities.

ŚRĪLA PRABHUPĀDA: Mm?

ŚYĀMASUNDARA: If we don't practice austerities voluntarily, then we must involuntarily practice some austerities.

ŚRĪLA PRABHUPĀDA: Yes, under the direction of the spiritual master one should... You have no mind to follow austerities, but when you accept a spiritual master, you have to carry out his order. That is austerity.

ŚYĀMASUNDARA: Even if you don't want to practice austerity, you must.

ŚRĪLA PRABHUPĀDA: Yes, you must. Because you have surrendered to your spiritual master, his order is final. So even if you don't like it, you have to do it. To please me.

ŚYĀMASUNDARA: Ah.

ŚRĪLA PRABHUPĀDA: But you don't like... [*He laughs.*] Nobody likes to fast, but the spiritual master says, "Today, fasting," so what can be done? [*Śyāmasundara laughs.*] A disciple is one who has voluntarily agreed to be disciplined by the spiritual master. That is austerity.

ŚYĀMASUNDARA: Say, like our parents or many people in the material world, completely enamored by the material life—they don't want to undergo austerity or bodily pain, but still they must. They are being forced by nature to suffer austerities.

ŚRĪLA PRABHUPĀDA: That is forced austerity. That is not good. Voluntary austerity will help.
ŚYĀMASUNDARA: If you don't undergo voluntary austerity, then you must be forced to undergo austerity.
ŚRĪLA PRABHUPĀDA: That is the difference between man and animal. An animal cannot accept austerity. But a man can accept it. There is a nice foodstuff in the confectioner's shop, so a man wants to eat it, but he sees that he has no money, so he can restrain himself. But when a cow comes, immediately she pushes her mouth in. You can beat her with a stick, but she will tolerate it. She will do that. Therefore an animal cannot undergo austerity. Our austerity is very nice. We chant Hare Kṛṣṇa, dance, and Kṛṣṇa sends very nice foodstuffs, and we eat. That's all. Why are your people not agreeable to such austerity? Chanting, dancing and eating nicely?
BOB: What is that?
ŚRĪLA PRABHUPĀDA: Because we are following austerities, Kṛṣṇa sends us nice things. So we are not losers. When you become Kṛṣṇa-ized, then you get *more* comforts than at the present moment. That's a fact. I have been living alone for the last twenty years, but I have no difficulties. Before taking *sannyāsa* I was living in Delhi. So I had no difficulties, although I was living alone.
ŚYĀMASUNDARA: If you don't accept spiritual discipline, then nature will force so many calamities.
ŚRĪLA PRABHUPĀDA: Oh, yes. That is stated in the *Bhagavad-gītā:*

daivī hy eṣā guṇa-mayī
mama māyā duratyayā
mām eva ye prapadyante
māyām etāṁ taranti te

["This divine energy of Mine, consisting of the three modes of material nature, is difficult to overcome. But those who have surrendered unto Me can easily cross beyond it."] *Māyā* is imposing so many difficulties, but as soon as you surrender to Kṛṣṇa, no more imposition.

ŚYĀMASUNDARA: We were so foolish that we were always thinking, "In the future I'll be happy."

ŚRĪLA PRABHUPĀDA: Yes, that is *māyā,* illusion. That is like the ass. You sit down on the back of the ass and just take a morsel of grass. The ass is thinking, "Let me go forward a little, and I shall get the grass." [*Bob laughs.*] But it is always one foot distant. That is ass-ism. [*They all laugh.*] Everyone is thinking, "Let me go a little forward, and I'll get it. I'll be very happy."

BOB: I... I thank you so much for...

ŚRĪLA PRABHUPĀDA: Hmm?

BOB: Tomorrow I'll have to leave you and—

ŚRĪLA PRABHUPĀDA: Don't talk l-e-a-v-e, but talk l-i-v-e.

BOB: I cannot yet, but I was thinking now of returning tomorrow to my town. But...

ŚRĪLA PRABHUPĀDA: Don't return.

BOB: I should stay here tomorrow—here?

ŚRĪLA PRABHUPĀDA: Stay here.

BOB: You tell me to, I'll stay.

ŚRĪLA PRABHUPĀDA: Yes, you are a very good boy. [*There is a long pause. It is now, much quieter.*] It is very simple. When the living entities forget Kṛṣṇa, they are in this material world. Kṛṣṇa means His name, His form, His abode, His pastimes—everything.

BOB: What was that last?

ŚRĪLA PRABHUPĀDA: Ah? Pastimes.

BOB: Pastimes.

ŚRĪLA PRABHUPĀDA: When we speak of a king, it means the king's government, king's palace, king's queen, king's sons, secretaries, military strength—everything. Is it not?
BOB: Yes.
ŚRĪLA PRABHUPĀDA: Similarly, Kṛṣṇa being the Supreme Personality of Godhead, as soon as we think of Kṛṣṇa, this means all the energies of Kṛṣṇa. That is complete by saying, "Rādhā-Kṛṣṇa." Rādhā represents all the energy of Kṛṣṇa. And Kṛṣṇa is the Supreme Lord. So when we speak of Kṛṣṇa, the living entities are also included because the living entities are energies, different energies of Kṛṣṇa—superior energy. So when this energy is not serving the energetic, that is material existence. The whole world is not serving Kṛṣṇa. They are serving Kṛṣṇa in a different way. They are serving indirectly, just as disobedient citizens serve the government indirectly. Prisoners come to the prison house on account of their disobedience of the laws of the state. So, in the prison house, they are forced to obey the laws of the state. Similarly, all the living entities here are godless, either by ignorance or by choice. They do not like to accept the supremacy of God. Demoniac. So we are trying to bring them to their original condition. That is the Kṛṣṇa consciousness movement.
BOB: I'd like to ask you just something I talked with devotees about—medicine. I walked to the river with some devotees today. I have a cold, so I said I shouldn't go in the water. Some felt I should because it is the Ganges, and some said I shouldn't because I have a cold, and we were talking, and I don't understand. Do we get sick because of our bad actions in the past?
ŚRĪLA PRABHUPĀDA: Yes, that's a fact.
BOB: But when one...

ŚRĪLA PRABHUPĀDA: Any kind of distress we suffer is due to our impious activities in the past.
BOB: But when someone is removed from karmic influence...
ŚRĪLA PRABHUPĀDA: Yes?
BOB: ... does he still get sick?
ŚRĪLA PRABHUPĀDA: No. Even if he gets sick, that is very temporary. For instance, this fan is moving. If you disconnect the electric power, then the fan will move for a moment. That movement is not due to the electric current. That is force—what is it called, physically, this force?
ŚYĀMASUNDARA: Momentum.
ŚRĪLA PRABHUPĀDA: Momentum. But as soon as it stops, no more movement. Similarly, even if a devotee who has surrendered to Kṛṣṇa is suffering from material consequences, that is temporary. Therefore, a devotee does not take any material miseries as miseries. He takes them as Kṛṣṇa's, God's, mercy.
BOB: A perfected soul, a devotee, a pure devotee...
ŚRĪLA PRABHUPĀDA: A perfected soul is one who engages twenty-four hours a day in Kṛṣṇa consciousness. That is perfection. That is a transcendental position. Perfection means to engage in one's original consciousness. That is perfection. That is stated in *Bhagavad-gītā:*

sve sve karmaṇy abhirataḥ
saṁsiddhiṁ labhate naraḥ

"By following his qualities of work, every man can become perfect." Complete perfection. *Saṁsiddhi. Siddhi* is perfection. That is Brahman realization, spiritual realization. And *saṁsiddhi* means devotion, which comes after Brahman realization.

BOB: Could you just say that last thing again please?
ŚRĪLA PRABHUPĀDA: *Saṁsiddhi.*
BOB: Yes.
ŚRĪLA PRABHUPĀDA: *Sam* means complete.
BOB: Yes.
ŚRĪLA PRABHUPĀDA: And *siddhi* means perfection. In the *Bhagavad-gītā* it is stated that one who goes back home, back to Godhead, has attained the complete perfection. So perfection comes when one realizes that he is not this body; he is spirit soul. *Brahma-bhūta*—that is called Brahman realization. That is perfection. And *saṁsiddhi* comes after Brahman realization, when one engages in devotional service. Therefore if one is already engaged in devotional service, it is to be understood that Brahman realization is there. Therefore it is called *saṁsiddhi.*
BOB: I ask you this very humbly, but do you feel diseases and sickness?
ŚRĪLA PRABHUPĀDA: Hm-m?
BOB: Do you personally feel disease and sickness?
ŚRĪLA PRABHUPĀDA: Yes.
BOB: Is this a result of your past *karma?*
ŚRĪLA PRABHUPĀDA: Yes.
BOB: So one in this material world never escapes his *karma* completely?
ŚRĪLA PRABHUPĀDA: Yes, he escapes. No more *karma* for a devotee. No more karmic reaction.
BOB: But you must be the best devotee.
ŚRĪLA PRABHUPĀDA: Hm-m... No, I don't consider myself the best devotee. I am the lowest.
BOB: No!
ŚRĪLA PRABHUPĀDA: *You* are the best devotee.
BOB: [*Laughs.*] Oh, no, no! But, see, you say—what you

say... always seems right.

ŚRĪLA PRABHUPĀDA: Yes.

BOB: Then you must be the best devotee.

ŚRĪLA PRABHUPĀDA: The thing is that even the best devotee, when he preaches, comes to the second-class platform of a devotee.

BOB: What would the best devotee be doing?

ŚRĪLA PRABHUPĀDA: The best devotee does not preach.

BOB: What does he do?

ŚRĪLA PRABHUPĀDA: He sees that there is no need of preaching. For him, everyone is a devotee. [*Bob laughs heartily*] Yes, he sees no more nondevotees—all devotees. He is called an *uttama-adhikārī*. But while I am preaching, how can I say I am the best devotee? Just like Rādhārāṇī—She does not see anyone as a nondevotee. Therefore we try to approach Rādhārāṇī.

BOB: Who is this?

ŚRĪLA PRABHUPĀDA: Rādhārāṇī, Kṛṣṇa's consort.

BOB: Ah.

ŚRĪLA PRABHUPĀDA: If anyone approaches Rādhārāṇī, She recommends to Kṛṣṇa, "Here is the best devotee. He is better than Me," and Kṛṣṇa cannot refuse him. That is the best devotee. But it is not to be imitated: "I have become the best devotee."

īśvare tad-adhīneṣu
bāliśeṣu dviṣatsu ca
prema-maitrī-kṛpopekṣā
yaḥ karoti sa madhyamaḥ
[Bhāg. 11.2.46]

A second-class devotee has the vision that some are envious of God, but this is not the vision of the best devotee.

The best devotee sees, "Nobody is envious of God. Everyone is better than me." Just like *Caitanya-caritāmṛta's* author, Kṛṣṇadāsa Kavirāja. He says, "I am lower than the worm in the stool."

BOB: Who is saying this?

ŚRĪLA PRABHUPĀDA: Kṛṣṇadāsa Kavirāja, the author of *Caitanya-caritāmṛta: purīṣera kīṭa haite muñi se laghiṣṭha.* He is not making a show. He is feeling like that. "I am the lowest. Everyone is best, but I am the lowest. Everyone is engaged in Kṛṣṇa's service. I am not engaged." Caitanya Mahāprabhu said "Oh, I have not a pinch of devotion to Kṛṣṇa. I cry to make a show. If I had been a devotee of Kṛṣṇa, I would have died long ago. But I am living. That is the proof that I do not love Kṛṣṇa." That is the vision of the best devotee. He is so much absorbed in Kṛṣṇa's love that he says, "Everything is going on, but I am the lowest. Therefore I cannot see God." That is the best devotee.

BOB: So a devotee must work for everybody's liberation?

ŚRĪLA PRABHUPĀDA: Yes. A devotee must work under the direction of a bona fide spiritual master, not imitate the best devotee.

BOB: Excuse me?

ŚRĪLA PRABHUPĀDA: One should not imitate the best devotee.

BOB: Imitate. Oh. I see.

ŚYĀMASUNDARA: One time you said that sometimes you feel sickness or pain due to the sinful activities of your devotees. Can sometimes disease be due to that? Caused by that?

ŚRĪLA PRABHUPĀDA: You see, Kṛṣṇa says:

ahaṁ tvāṁ sarva-pāpebhyo
mokṣayiṣyāmi mā śucaḥ

"I will deliver you from all sinful reaction. Do not fear." So Kṛṣṇa is so powerful that He can immediately take up all the sins of others and immediately make them right. But when a living entity plays the part on behalf of Kṛṣṇa, he also takes the responsibility for the sinful activities of his devotees. Therefore to become a *guru* is not an easy task. You see? He has to take all the poisons and absorb them. So sometimes—because he is not Kṛṣṇa—sometimes there is some trouble. Therefore Caitanya Mahāprabhu has forbidden, "Don't make many *śiṣyas,* many disciples." But for preaching work we have to accept many disciples—for expanding preaching—even if we suffer. That's a fact. The spiritual master has to take the responsibility for all the sinful activities of his disciples. Therefore to make many disciples is a risky job unless one is able to assimilate all the sins.

vāñchā-kalpa-tarubhyaś ca
kṛpā-sindhubhya eva ca
patitānāṁ pāvanebhyo
vaiṣṇavebhyo namo namaḥ

["I offer my respectful obeisances unto all the Vaiṣṇava devotees of the Lord. They are just like desire trees who can fulfill the desires of everyone, and they are full of compassion for the fallen conditioned souls."] He takes responsibility for all the fallen souls. That idea is also in the Bible. Jesus Christ took all the sinful reactions of the people and sacrificed his life. That is the responsibility of a spiritual master. Because Kṛṣṇa is Kṛṣṇa, He is *apāpa-viddha*—He cannot be attacked by sinful reactions. But a living entity is sometimes subjected to their influence because he is so small. Big fire, small fire. If you put some big thing in a small fire, the fire itself may be extinguished. But in a big fire, whatever you put in is all right. The big fire can consume anything.

BOB: Christ's suffering was of that nature?

ŚRĪLA PRABHUPĀDA: Mm-m?

BOB: Was Christ's suffering—

ŚRĪLA PRABHUPĀDA: That I have already explained. He took the sinful reactions of all the people. Therefore he suffered.

BOB: I see.

ŚRĪLA PRABHUPĀDA: He said—that is in the Bible—that he took all the sinful reactions of the people and sacrificed his life. But these Christian people have made it a law for Christ to suffer while they do all nonsense. [*Bob gives a short laugh.*] Such great fools they are! They have let Jesus Christ make a contract for taking all their sinful reactions so they can go on with all nonsense. That is their religion. Christ was so magnanimous that he took all their sins and suffered, but that does not induce them to *stop* all these sins. They have not come to that sense. They have taken it very easily. "Let Lord Jesus Christ suffer, and we'll do all nonsense." Is it not?

BOB: It is so.

ŚRĪLA PRABHUPĀDA: They should have been ashamed: "Lord Jesus Christ suffered for us, but we are continuing the sinful activities." He told everyone, "Thou shalt not kill," but they are indulging in killing, thinking, "Lord Jesus Christ will excuse us and take all the sinful reactions." This is going on. We should be very much cautious: "For my sinful actions my spiritual master will suffer, so I'll not commit even a pinch of sinful activities." That is the duty of the disciple. After initiation, all sinful reaction is finished. Now if he again commits sinful activities, his spiritual master has to suffer. A disciple should be sympathetic and consider this. "For my sinful activities, my spiritual master will suffer." If the spiritual master is attacked by some disease, it is due to the sinful activities of others. "Don't make many disciples." But we do it because we are preaching. Never mind—let us suffer—still we shall accept them. Therefore your question was—when I suffer is it due to my past misdeeds? Was it not? *That* is my misdeed—that I accepted some disciples who are nonsense. That is my misdeed.

BOB: This happens on occasions?

ŚRĪLA PRABHUPĀDA: Yes. This is sure to happen because we are accepting so many men. It is the duty of the disciples to be cautious. "My spiritual master has saved me. I should not put him again into suffering." When the spiritual master is in suffering, Kṛṣṇa saves him. Kṛṣṇa thinks, "Oh, he has taken so much responsibility for delivering a fallen person." So Kṛṣṇa is there.

kaunteya pratijānīhi
na me bhaktaḥ praṇaśyati

["O son of Kuntī, declare it boldly that My devotee never perishes."] Because the spiritual master takes the risk on account of Kṛṣṇa.

BOB: Your suffering is not the same kind of pain...

ŚRĪLA PRABHUPĀDA: No, it is not due to *karma*. The pain is there sometimes, so that the disciples may know, "Due to our sinful activities, our spiritual master is suffering."

BOB: You look very well now.

ŚRĪLA PRABHUPĀDA: I am always well... in the sense that

even if there is suffering, I know Kṛṣṇa will protect me. But this suffering is not due to *my* sinful activities.

BOB: But let us say when I—in the town I live in, I take boiled water because some of the water has disease in it. Now, why should I drink boiled water if I have been good enough not to get a disease? Then I may drink any water. And if I have been not acting properly, then I shall get disease anyway.

ŚRĪLA PRABHUPĀDA: So long as you are in the material world, you cannot neglect physical laws. Suppose you go to a jungle and there is a tiger. It is known that it will attack you, so why should you voluntarily go and be attacked? It is not that a devotee should take physical risk so long as he has a physical body. It is not a challenge to the physical laws: "I have become a devotee. I challenge everything." That is foolishness.

anāsaktasya viṣayān
yathārham upayuñjataḥ
nirbandhaḥ kṛṣṇa-sambandhe
yuktaṁ vairāgyam ucyate

The devotee is advised to accept the necessities of life without attachment. He'll take boiled water, but if boiled water is not available, does it mean he will not drink water? If it is not available, he will drink ordinary water. We take Kṛṣṇa *prasāda,* but while touring, sometimes we have to take some food in a hotel. Because one is a devotee, should he think, "I will not take any foodstuffs from the hotel. I shall starve"? If I starve, then I will be weak and will not be able to preach.

BOB: Does a devotee lose some of his individuality, in that—

ŚRĪLA PRABHUPĀDA: No, he has full individuality for pleasing Kṛṣṇa. Kṛṣṇa says, "You surrender unto Me." So he voluntarily surrenders. It is not that he has lost his individuality. He keeps his individuality. Just like Arjuna—in the beginning, he was declining to fight, on account of his individuality. But when he accepted Kṛṣṇa as his spiritual master, he became *śiṣya* [a disciple]. Then whatever Kṛṣṇa ordered, he said yes. That doesn't mean he lost his individuality. He voluntarily accepted: "Whatever Kṛṣṇa says, I shall do it." Just like all my disciples—they have not lost their individuality, but they have surrendered their individuality. That is required. For example, suppose a man does not use sex. It does not mean he has become impotent. If he likes, he can have sex life a thousand times. But he has voluntarily avoided it. *Paraṁ dṛṣṭvā nivartate:* he has a higher taste. Sometimes we fast, but that does not mean we are diseased. We voluntarily fast. It does not mean that I am not hungry or cannot eat. But we voluntarily fast.

BOB: Does the devotee who surrenders keep his individual taste?

ŚRĪLA PRABHUPĀDA: Yes, in full.

BOB: Taste for different things?

ŚRĪLA PRABHUPĀDA: Hm?

BOB: Does he keep his individual likes and dislikes?

ŚRĪLA PRABHUPĀDA: Yes, he keeps everything. But he gives preference to Kṛṣṇa. Suppose I like this thing but Kṛṣṇa says, "No, you cannot use it." Then I shall not use it. It is for Kṛṣṇa's sake.

nirbandhaḥ kṛṣṇa-sambandhe
yuktaṁ vairāgyam ucyate

Kṛṣṇa says positively, "I like these things." So we have to

offer to Kṛṣṇa what He likes, and then we'll take *prasāda.* Kṛṣṇa likes Rādhārāṇī. Therefore all the *gopīs,* they are trying to push Rādhārāṇī to Kṛṣṇa. "Kṛṣṇa likes this *gopī.* All right, push Her." That is Kṛṣṇa consciousness. To satisfy the senses of Kṛṣṇa, not to satisfy my senses. That is *bhakti.* That is called *prema,* love for Kṛṣṇa. "Ah, Kṛṣṇa likes this. I must give Him this."

BOB: There is some *prasāda* [food offered to Kṛṣṇa]. It's offered, and then we go and eat, and different *prasādams* are served. Some I like, and some I find the taste not at all to my liking.

ŚRĪLA PRABHUPĀDA: You should not do that. The perfection is that whatever is offered to Kṛṣṇa you should accept. That is perfection. You cannot say, "I like this, I don't like this." So long as you make such discrimination, that means you have not appreciated what *prasāda* is.

A DEVOTEE: What if there is someone speaking of likes and dislikes? Say someone is preparing some *prasāda*...

ŚRĪLA PRABHUPĀDA: No disliking, no liking. Whatever Kṛṣṇa likes, that's all right.

A DEVOTEE: Yes. But say someone prepares something, like some *prasāda* for Kṛṣṇa, but he does not make it so good, and it is—

ŚRĪLA PRABHUPĀDA: No, if made sincerely with devotion, then Kṛṣṇa will like it. Just like Vidu. Vidu was feeding Kṛṣṇa bananas, but he was so absorbed in thought that he was throwing away the real bananas and he was giving Kṛṣṇa the skin, and Kṛṣṇa was eating. [*All laugh*] Kṛṣṇa knew that he was giving in devotion, and Kṛṣṇa can eat anything, provided there is devotion. It does not matter whether it is materially tasteful or not. Similarly, a devotee also takes Kṛṣṇa *prasāda,* whether it is materially tasteful or not. We should accept everything.

A DEVOTEE: But if the devotion is not there, like in India...

ŚRĪLA PRABHUPĀDA: If devotion is not there, He doesn't like any food, either tasteful or not tasteful. He does not accept it.

A DEVOTEE: In India... Somebody—

ŚRĪLA PRABHUPĀDA: Oh, India, India. Don't talk of India! Talk of philosophy. If there is not devotion, Kṛṣṇa does not accept anything, either in India or in your country. Lord Kṛṣṇa is not obliged to accept anything costly because it is very tasty. Kṛṣṇa has very many tasteful dishes in Vaikuṇṭha. He is not hankering after your food. He accepts your devotion, *bhakti*. The real thing is devotion, not the food. Kṛṣṇa does not accept any food of this material world. He accepts only the devotion.

patraṁ puṣpaṁ phalaṁ toyaṁ
yo me bhaktyā prayacchati
tad ahaṁ bhakty-upahṛtam
aśnāmi prayatātmanaḥ

["If one offers Me with love and devotion a leaf, a flower, fruit or water, I will accept it."] "Because it has been offered to Me with devotion and love"—that is required. Therefore we do not allow anyone to cook who is not a devotee. Kṛṣṇa does not accept anything from the hands of a nondevotee. Why should He accept? He is not hungry. He does not require any food. He accepts only the devotion, that's all. That is the main point. So one has to become a devotee. Not a good cook. But if he is a devotee, then he will be a good cook also. Automatically he will become a good cook. Therefore one has to become a devotee only. Then all other good qualifications will automatically be there. And if he is a nondevotee, any good qualifications have no value. He is on the mental plane, so he has no good qualification. [*There is a long pause in the conversation.*]

ŚRĪLA PRABHUPĀDA: And the time?

ŚYĀMASUNDARA: Six o'clock.

ŚRĪLA PRABHUPĀDA: Questions and answers are required. They are beneficial to all.

BOB: I still have a question on the *prasāda.*

ŚRĪLA PRABHUPĀDA: Sūta Gosvāmī says:

munayaḥ sādhu pṛṣṭo 'haṁ
bhavadbhir loka-maṅgalam
yat kṛtaḥ kṛṣṇa-sampraśno
yenātmā suprasīdati

["O sages, I have been justly questioned by you. Your questions are worthy because they relate to Lord Kṛṣṇa and so are relevant to the world's welfare. Only questions of this sort are capable of completely satisfying the self."] *Kṛṣṇa-sampraśnaḥ,* that is very good. When you discuss and hear, that is *loka-maṅgalam,* auspicious for everyone. Both the questions and the answers.

BOB: I still do not understand so much about *prasāda.* But if you like I'll think about it and ask you again tomorrow.

ŚRĪLA PRABHUPĀDA: *Prasāda* is always *prasāda.* But because we are not elevated sufficiently, therefore we do not like some *prasāda.*

BOB: I found specifically that what I mean—that some are too spicy, and it hurts my stomach.

ŚRĪLA PRABHUPĀDA: Well... That is also due to not appreciating, but the cook should have consideration. Kṛṣṇa must be offered first-class foodstuffs. So if he offers something last class, he is not performing his duty. But Kṛṣṇa can accept anything if it is offered by a devotee, and a devotee can accept any *prasāda,* even if it is spicy. Hiraṇyakaśipu gave his son poison [and the son offered it to Kṛṣṇa], and the son drank it as nectar. So even if it is spicy to others' taste, it is very palatable to the devotee. What is the question of spicy? He was offered poison, real poison. And Pūtanā Rākṣasī—she also offered Kṛṣṇa poison. But Kṛṣṇa is so nice that He thought, "She took Me as My mother," so He took the poison and delivered her. Kṛṣṇa does not take the bad side. A good man does not take the bad side—he takes only the good side. Just like one of my big Godbrothers—he wanted to make business with my Guru Mahārāja [spiritual master], but my Guru Mahārāja did not take the bad side. He took the good side. He thought, "He has come forward to give me some service."

BOB: Business with your—what was that? Business with who?

ŚRĪLA PRABHUPĀDA: I am talking about my Guru Mahārāja.

BOB: Oh, I see. I have another question on *prasāda,* if I may. Let us say some devotee has some trouble and does not eat a certain type of food—like some devotees do not eat ghee because of liver trouble. So these devotees, should they take all the *prasāda?*

ŚRĪLA PRABHUPĀDA: No, no. Those who are not perfect devotees may discriminate. But a perfect devotee does not discriminate. Why should you imitate a perfect devotee? So long as you have discrimination, you are not a perfect devotee. So why should you artificially imitate a perfect devotee and eat everything?

BOB: Oh.

ŚRĪLA PRABHUPĀDA: The point is, a perfect devotee does not make any discrimination. Whatever is offered to Kṛṣṇa is nectar. That's all. Kṛṣṇa accepts anything from a devotee. "Whatever is offered to Me by My devotee," He accepts. The same thing for a devotee. Don't you see the point? A perfect devotee does not make any discrimination. But if I am not a perfect devotee and I have discrimination, why shall I imitate the perfect devotee? It may not be possible for me to digest everything because I am not a perfect devotee. A devotee should not be a foolish man. It is said:

kṛṣṇa ye bhaje se baḍa catura

So a devotee knows his position, and he is intelligent enough to deal with others accordingly.

SEVEN

Acting in Knowledge of Kṛṣṇa February 29, 1972 (evening, continued)

AN INDIAN GENTLEMAN: By what kind of actions does one earn good *karma?*

ŚRĪLA PRABHUPĀDA: Good *karma* means what is prescribed in the *Vedas.* Specifically, it is prescribed that one should perform *yajña. Yajña* means actions for the satisfaction of Lord Viṣṇu, the Supreme Personality of Godhead. So good *karma* means performance of the *yajñas* as they are prescribed in the Vedic literatures. And the purpose of this *yajña* is to satisfy the Supreme Lord. A good, law-abiding citizen is one whose actions satisfy the government. So, good *karma* is to satisfy Lord Viṣṇu, the Supreme Lord. Unfortunately, modern civilization does not know what the Supreme Personality of Godhead is, what to speak of satisfying Him. People do not know. They are simply busy with material activities. Therefore all of them are performing only bad *karma* and therefore suffering. They are blind men leading other blind men. And both are then suffering by bad *karma.* That is very easy to understand. If you do something criminal, you will suffer. If you do something benevolent for the state, for the people, then you are recognized; you are sometimes given a title. This is good and bad *karma.* So, good *karma* means you enjoy some material happiness; bad *karma* means you suffer from material distress. By good *karma* you get birth in a good family; you get riches, good money. Then you become a learned scholar; you become beautiful also.

[*Some time passes.*]

BOB: What about the person who—who is not very aware of God, but...

ŚRĪLA PRABHUPĀDA: Then he is an animal. The animal does not know what is good. A person who does not know what is God, or one who does not try to understand what is God—he is an animal. The animals are with four legs, and that animal is with two legs. And Darwin's theory is they are monkeys. So anyone who does not know God, or does not try to understand God, is nothing but an animal.

BOB: What about the innocent people?

ŚRĪLA PRABHUPĀDA: The animal is very innocent. If you cut its throat, it won't protest. So innocence is not a very good qualification. The animals are all innocent. Therefore you get the chance to cut their throats. So to become innocent is not a very good qualification. Our proposition is that one must be very, very intelligent, and then he can understand Kṛṣṇa. To become an innocent, ignorant simpleton is not a very good qualification. Simplicity is all right, but one should not be unintelligent.

BOB: Can you tell me again what intelligence is?

ŚRĪLA PRABHUPĀDA: Intelligence means... One who knows what he is, what is this world, what is God, what are the interrelations—he is intelligent. The animal does not know what he is. He thinks that he is the body. Similarly, anyone who does not know what he is, he is not intelligent.

BOB: What about a person who does—tries to do—what is right and is very conscientious instead of being unconscious about the things he does? Like the servant who is very honest to his master but knows that if he were not

honest he would not be caught. If he stays honest anyway... a person like that? Is that some kind of good *karma?*
ŚRĪLA PRABHUPĀDA: Yes, to become honest is also good *karma.* How to become a good man is described in the *Bhagavad-gītā* very elaborately.

daivī sampad vimokṣāya
nibandhāyāsurī matā

So if you become qualified with the *daivī sampad* (transcendental qualities), then, *vimokṣāya*—you will be liberated. And, *nibandhāyāsurī*—if you are qualified with the demoniac qualifications, then you will be more and more entangled. Unfortunately the modern civilization does not know what is liberation and what is entanglement. They are so much ignorant; they do not know. Suppose if I ask you what you mean by liberation, can you answer? [*No answer.*] And if I ask you what you mean by entanglement, can you answer? [*Again no answer.*] These words are there in the Vedic literature—liberation and entanglement—but, at the present moment, people do not even know what is liberation and what is entanglement. They are so ignorant and foolish, and still they are proud of their advancement in knowledge. Can you answer what is liberation? You are a professor, teacher, but if I ask you, can you explain what is liberation?
BOB: Not adequately because if I could explain, then I would become liberated very fast.
ŚRĪLA PRABHUPĀDA: But if you do not know what is liberation, then how fast or slow liberation? [*Everyone laughs.*] There is no question of liberation. It is neither fast nor slow. You should first know what is liberation. If you do not know where the train is going, then what is the use

of asking, understanding, whether it is going fast or slow? You do not know your destination. What is liberation?

BOB: Umm...

ŚRĪLA PRABHUPĀDA: I am asking. You daily ask me. I am asking *you.*

BOB: [*Laughs.*] Ah—okay... I'll think for a moment.

ŚRĪLA PRABHUPĀDA: Liberation is described in the *Śrīmad-Bhāgavatam.* The exact Sanskrit word for liberation is *mukti.* So that is defined in the *Śrīmad-Bhāgavatam.*

muktir hitvānyathā rūpaṁ
svarūpena vyavasthitiḥ

One should stop doing all nonsense, and he must be situated in his original position. But this is also more embarrassing because nobody knows his original position and how to act properly. Because people are generally acting differently, because they do not know what is proper—the modern population is so much ignorant about their life—it is a very awkward position. They do not know.

BOB: Can you tell me who is honest?

ŚRĪLA PRABHUPĀDA: If one does not know what is honesty, how can he be honest? But if you know what is honesty, then you can be honest. What is honesty? First of all explain.

BOB: Aaah, ummm—Honesty is doing what you really feel is right.

ŚRĪLA PRABHUPĀDA: A thief is feeling, "I must steal to provide for my children. It is right." Does it mean that he is honest? Everyone thinks—The butcher thinks, "It is my life. I must cut the throat of the animals daily." Just like that—what is that hunter? And Nārada Muni met him?

ŚYĀMASUNDARA: Mṛgāri.

ŚRĪLA PRABHUPĀDA: Yes, Mṛgāri. Nārada asked him, "Why are you killing in this way?" And he said, "Oh, it is my business. My father taught it." So he was honestly doing that. So a feeling of honesty depends on culture. A thief's culture is different. He thinks stealing is honest.

BOB: So what is honesty?

ŚRĪLA PRABHUPĀDA: Yes, that is my question. [*Everyone laughs.*] Real honesty is that you should not encroach upon another's property. This is honesty. For instance, this is my table. If you want to take it away while going, is that honesty? So therefore the simple definition of honesty is that you should not encroach upon another's rights. That is honesty.

BOB: So somebody who is honest would be in the mode of goodness? Would that be correct?

ŚRĪLA PRABHUPĀDA: Certainly, certainly. Because the mode of goodness means knowledge. So if you know, "This table does not belong to me; it belongs to Swāmījī," you will not try to take it away. Therefore, one must know—be thoroughly well conversant—then he can be honest.

BOB: So, now you have said the mode of goodness was knowledge of God, but somebody may be honest without having very much knowledge of God.

ŚRĪLA PRABHUPĀDA: Hm-m?

BOB: Without—without being honest—without thinking they are honest because it is God's wishes—they just feel like they ought to be honest.

ŚRĪLA PRABHUPĀDA: Mmm. God wishes everyone to be honest. Why should God think otherwise?

BOB: So... so you may follow God's wishes without knowing you are following God's wishes? Like somebody may be in the mode...

ŚRĪLA PRABHUPĀDA: No, following without knowing—that is absurd. You must know the order of God. And if you follow that, then that is honesty.

BOB: But somebody would not be honest without knowing God?

ŚRĪLA PRABHUPĀDA: Yes, because God is the supreme proprietor, the supreme enjoyer, and He is the supreme friend. That is the statement of the *Bhagavad-gītā*. If anyone knows these three things, then he is in full knowledge. These three things only: that God is the proprietor of everything, God is friend of everyone, and God is the enjoyer of everything. For example, everyone knows that in the body, the stomach is the enjoyer. Not the hands, legs, eyes, ears. These are there simply to help the stomach. Eyes—the vulture goes seven miles up to see where there is food for the stomach. Is it not?

BOB: That is so.

ŚRĪLA PRABHUPĀDA: Then the wings fly there, and the jaws catch the food. Similarly, as in this body the stomach is the enjoyer, the central figure of the whole cosmic manifestation, material or spiritual, is Kṛṣṇa, God. He is the enjoyer. We can understand this just by considering our own bodies. The body is also a creation. The body has the same mechanical nature you will find in the whole universe. The same mechanical arrangement will be found anywhere you go, even in animals. In the human body or in the cosmic manifestation—almost the same mechanism. So you can understand very easily that in this body—my body, your body—the stomach is the enjoyer. There is a central enjoyer. And the stomach is the friend also. Because if you cannot digest food, you see, then all other limbs of the body become weak. Therefore the stomach is the friend. It is digesting and distributing the energy to all the limbs of the body. Is it not?

BOB: It is so.

ŚRĪLA PRABHUPĀDA: Similarly, the central stomach of the whole creation is God, or Kṛṣṇa. He is the enjoyer, He is the friend, and, as the supreme proprietor, He is maintaining everyone. Just as a king can maintain the whole country's citizens because he is the proprietor. Without being the proprietor, how can one become everyone's friend? So these things have to be understood. Kṛṣṇa is the enjoyer, Kṛṣṇa is the proprietor, and Kṛṣṇa is the friend. If you know these three things, then your knowledge is full; you do not require to understand anything more.

yasmin vijñāte sarvam evaṁ vijñātaṁ bhavati

If you simply understand Kṛṣṇa by these three formulas, then your knowledge is complete. You don't require any more knowledge. But people will not agree. "Why should Kṛṣṇa be the proprietor? Hitler should be the proprietor. Nixon..." That is going on. Therefore you are in trouble. But if you understand these three things only, then your knowledge is complete. But you will not accept—you will put forward so many impediments to understanding these three things, and that is the cause of our trouble. But in the *Bhagavad-gītā* it is plainly said:

bhoktāraṁ yajña-tapasāṁ
sarva-loka-maheśvaram
suhṛdaṁ sarva-bhūtānāṁ
jñātvā māṁ śāntim ṛcchati

["The sages, knowing Me as the ultimate purpose of all

sacrifices and austerities, the Supreme Lord of all planets and demigods and the benefactor and well-wisher of all living entities, attain peace from the pangs of material miseries."] But we won't take this. We shall put forward so many false proprietors, false friends, false enjoyers, and they will fight one another. This is the situation of the world. If education is given and people take this knowledge, there is immediately peace (*śāntim ṛcchati*). This is knowledge, and if anyone follows this principle, he is honest. He does not claim, "It is mine." He knows everything: "Oh, it is Kṛṣṇa's, so therefore everything should be utilized for Kṛṣṇa's service." That is honesty. If this pencil belongs to me, the etiquette is—My students sometimes ask, "Can I use this pencil?" "Yes, you can." Similarly, if I know that everything belongs to Kṛṣṇa, I will not use anything without His permission. That is honesty. And that is knowledge. One who does not know is ignorant; he is foolish. And a foolish man commits criminality. All criminals are foolish men. Out of ignorance one commits lawbreaking. So ignorance is not bliss, but it is folly to be wise where ignorance is bliss. That is the difficulty. The whole world is enjoying ignorance. And when you talk about Kṛṣṇa consciousness, they do not very much appreciate it. If I say, "Kṛṣṇa is the proprietor; you are not the proprietor," you will not be very much satisfied. [*They laugh.*] Just see—ignorance is bliss. So it is my foolishness to say the real truth. Therefore it is folly to be wise where ignorance is bliss. So we are taking the risk of offending people, and they will think we are fools. If I say to a rich man, "You are not the proprietor, Kṛṣṇa is the proprietor, so whatever money you have, spend it for Kṛṣṇa," he will be angry.

upadeśo hi mūrkhānāṁ
prakopāya na śāntaye

"If you instruct a rascal, he'll be angry." Therefore we go as beggars: "My dear sir, you are a very nice man. I am a *sannyāsī* beggar, so I want to construct a temple. Can you spare some money?" So he will think, "Oh, here is a beggar. Give him some money." [*They laugh*] But if I say, "Dear sir, you have millions of dollars at your disposal. That is Kṛṣṇa's money. Give it to me. I am Kṛṣṇa's servant." Oh, he'll... [*Everyone laughs.*] He will not be very satisfied. Rather, if I go as a beggar, he will give me something. And if I tell him the truth, he will not give me a farthing. [*They laugh*] We convince him as beggars. We are not beggars. We are Kṛṣṇa's servants. We don't want anything from anyone. Because we know Kṛṣṇa will provide everything.

BOB: Oh-h...

ŚRĪLA PRABHUPĀDA: This is knowledge. For instance, a child will sometimes take something important, so we have to flatter him. "Oh, you are so nice. Please take these lozenges and give me that paper. It is nothing; it is paper." And he will say, "Oh, yes. Take. That's nice." Two-paise lozenges—very nice and sweet. So we have to do that. Why? Because a man will go to hell by taking Kṛṣṇa's money. So some way or other, take some money from him and engage him in the Kṛṣṇa consciousness movement.

BOB: And then he may not go to hell?

ŚRĪLA PRABHUPĀDA: Yes. You save him from going to hell. Because a farthing spent for Kṛṣṇa will be accounted: "Oh, this man has given a farthing." This is called *ajñāta-sukṛti* [spiritual activity one performs unknowingly]. They are very poor in their thought. Therefore the saintly persons move just to enlighten them a little. To give them a chance. Giving them a chance to serve Kṛṣṇa. That is the saintly person's duty.

BOB: That is what?

ŚRĪLA PRABHUPĀDA: That is his duty. But if he takes money from others and utilizes it for his sense gratification, then he goes to hell. Then it is finished. Then he is a cheater; actually he is a criminal. You cannot take money, a farthing, from anyone, and use it for your own sense gratification.

BOB: I think of people I know who are not Kṛṣṇa conscious.

ŚRĪLA PRABHUPĀDA: Kṛṣṇa means God.

BOB: They are just slightly God conscious, but still these people are honest to the extent that they don't take from other people at all. And they try to be honest with other people. Will these—

ŚRĪLA PRABHUPĀDA: He does not take from other people, but he takes from God.

BOB: So these people are half-good?

ŚRĪLA PRABHUPĀDA: Hm-m?

BOB: These people are then half-good?

ŚRĪLA PRABHUPĀDA: Not good. If he does not learn this principle—that God is the proprietor... Others' things? What do you mean, "others' things"?

BOB: Like, people I'm thinking of—they're poor people who need money and food but—

ŚRĪLA PRABHUPĀDA: Everyone needs money. Everyone needs it. Who is not poor? There are so many gentlemen sitting here. Who is not in need of money and food? You are also in need of money. So how do you distinguish poor from rich? Everyone needs it. If that is your definition...

If one needs money and food, then everyone needs money and food. So everyone is poor.

BOB: So, but, well—I was thinking in terms of just people who are relatively poor.

ŚRĪLA PRABHUPĀDA: Relatively, relatively, maybe. You are more hungry than me. That does not mean you are not hungry or I am not hungry. I do not feel hungry now. That does not mean I do not feel hungry or I am not hungry. For the time being you may not be hungry. But tomorrow you'll be hungry.

BOB: What I feel is that—somehow these people—that... Everybody around them may be stealing, but they still stand up and don't steal. These people somehow deserve something good to happen to them.

ŚRĪLA PRABHUPĀDA: But the man who is thinking that he is not stealing is also a thief because he does not know that everything belongs to Kṛṣṇa. Therefore, whatever he is accepting, he is stealing.

BOB: Is he less of a thief?

ŚRĪLA PRABHUPĀDA: You may not know that I am the proprietor of this wrapper, but if you take it away, are you not stealing?

BOB: But maybe if I know it is yours and I take it, I am a worse thief than if I do not know whose it is. I just think it may be nobody's, and I take it.

ŚRĪLA PRABHUPĀDA: That is also stealing. Because it must belong to somebody. And you take it without his permission. You may not know exactly who is the proprietor, but you know, "It must belong to someone." That is knowledge. Sometimes we see on the road so many valuable things left there—government property for repairing roads or some electrical work. A man may think,

"Oh, fortunately these things are lying here, so I may take them." Is it not stealing?

BOB: It is stealing.

ŚRĪLA PRABHUPĀDA: Yes. He does not know that this is all government property. He takes it away. That is stealing. And when he is caught, he is arrested, and he is punished. So, similarly, whatever you are collecting—suppose you are drinking a glass of water from the river. Is the river your property?

BOB: No.

ŚRĪLA PRABHUPĀDA: Then? It is stealing. You have not created the river. You do not know who is the proprietor. Therefore it is not your property. So, even if you drink a glass of water without knowing to whom it belongs, you are a thief. So you may think, "I am honest," but actually you are a thief. You must remember Kṛṣṇa. "Oh, Kṛṣṇa, it is Your creation, so kindly allow me to drink." This is honesty. Therefore a devotee always thinks of Kṛṣṇa. In all activities: "Oh, it is Kṛṣṇa's." This is honesty. So without Kṛṣṇa consciousness, everyone is a rascal, is a thief, is a rogue, is a robber. These qualifications. Therefore our conclusion is that anyone who does not understand Kṛṣṇa has no good qualifications. Neither is he honest, nor has he knowledge. Therefore he is a third-class man. Is that correct? What do you think, Girirāja?

GIRIRĀJA [a disciple]: Yes.

ŚRĪLA PRABHUPĀDA: This is not dogmatism. This is a fact. [*Some time elapses.*] So, you have understood what is knowledge and what is honesty?

BOB: I—in a way. In a way.

ŚRĪLA PRABHUPĀDA: And is there another way? [*Bob laughs.*] Is there any other way? Defy it! [*Bob laughs again.*

Śrīla Prabhupāda also laughs.] Another way? Girirāja?

GIRIRĀJA: No.

ŚRĪLA PRABHUPĀDA: Is there an alternative? We do not say anything that can be defied by anyone. That experience we have. Rather, we defy everyone: "Any questions?" Till now, Kṛṣṇa has given us protection. In big, big meetings in big, big countries, after speaking I ask, "Any questions?"

BOB: Now, I have none.

ŚRĪLA PRABHUPĀDA: In London, we had—how many days' lectures in that—what is that? Conway Hall?

A DEVOTEE: Twelve days. Conway Hall.

ŚRĪLA PRABHUPĀDA: Conway Hall.

A DEVOTEE: Twelve days.

ŚRĪLA PRABHUPĀDA: Yes. So after every meeting I was asking, "Any questions?"

BOB: Did you get many questions?

ŚRĪLA PRABHUPĀDA: Oh, yes. Many foolish questions. [*Everyone laughs.*]

BOB: Let me ask one more question. What is being foolish?

ŚRĪLA PRABHUPĀDA: One having no knowledge is to be considered foolish.

AN INDIAN GENTLEMAN: Prabhupāda, I have one personal question. Can I ask?

ŚRĪLA PRABHUPĀDA: Yes.

INDIAN GENTLEMAN: Some time ago in Calcutta they observed a week—it was named, "Prevention of Cruelty to Animals Week."

ŚRĪLA PRABHUPĀDA: Mmm. [*He gives a quick laugh*] This is another foolishness. They are advertising prevention of cruelty, and they are maintaining thousands of slaughterhouses. You see? That is another foolishness.

INDIAN GENTLEMAN: So I wanted just to ask—

ŚRĪLA PRABHUPĀDA: Asking—before you ask, I give you the answer. [*All laugh*] That is another foolishness. They are regularly cruel to animals, and they are making a society...

BOB: Maybe this is—

ŚRĪLA PRABHUPĀDA: Suppose a gang of thieves has a signboard—"Goodman and Company." You sometimes find such a signboard.

ŚYĀMASUNDARA: Our landlord in the San Francisco temple was named Goodman.

ŚRĪLA PRABHUPĀDA: The philosophy is that when an animal is not properly nourished, that is cruelty. Therefore instead of allowing it to starve, better to kill it. That is their theory. Is it not?

BOB: Yes.

ŚRĪLA PRABHUPĀDA: They say, "Oh, it is better to kill him than to give him so much pain." That theory is coming in communist countries. An old man—grandfather—is suffering, so better to kill him. And there—in Africa there is a class of men who make a festival by killing their great-grandfathers. Is it not? Yes.

ŚYĀMASUNDARA: They eat them?

ŚRĪLA PRABHUPĀDA: Yes. [*Śyāmasundara laughs.*] Yes?

A DEVOTEE: I had an uncle and aunt. They were in the Army. So when they went overseas, they could not take their dog with them. So they said, "The poor dog. He will be so heartbroken not to be with us," so they put him to sleep—killed him.

ŚRĪLA PRABHUPĀDA: In Gandhi's life also, he once killed one calf or some cow. It was suffering very much. So

Gandhi ordered, "Instead of letting it suffer, just kill it."

GIRIRĀJA: Yesterday you said that the spiritual master may have to suffer due to the sinful activities of his disciples. What do you mean by sinful activities?

ŚRĪLA PRABHUPĀDA: Sinful activities means that you promised, "I shall follow the regulative principles." If you do not follow, that is sinful. That is the promise. Very simple. You break the promise and do nasty things; therefore you are sinful. Is it not?

GIRIRĀJA: Yes. [*pause*] But there are some things that we're instructed to do...

ŚRĪLA PRABHUPĀDA: Hm-m?

GIRIRĀJA: There are other things which we're instructed to do which, even though we try to do, we cannot do perfectly yet.

ŚRĪLA PRABHUPĀDA: How is that? You try to do and cannot do? How is that?

GIRIRĀJA: Like chanting attentively. Sometimes we try to, but—

ŚRĪLA PRABHUPĀDA: Well, that is not a fault. Suppose you are trying to do something. Due to your inexperience if you sometimes fail, that is not a fault. You are trying. There is a verse in the *Bhāgavatam*—hm-m—that if a devotee is trying his best but due to his incapability he sometimes fails, Kṛṣṇa excuses him. And in the *Bhagavad-gītā* also it is said:

api cet su-durācāro
bhajate mām ananya-bhāk

Sometimes not willingly but due to past bad habits—habit is second nature—one does something nonsensical. But that does not mean he is faulty. But he must repent for that—"I have done this." And he should try to avoid it as far as possible. But habit is second nature. Sometimes, in spite of your trying hard, *māyā* is so strong that it pushes with pitfalls. That can be excused. Kṛṣṇa excuses. But those who are doing something willingly are not excused. On the strength that I am a devotee, if I think, "Because I am chanting, I may therefore commit all this nonsense, and it will be nullified," that is the greatest offense.

EIGHT

Advancing in Kṛṣṇa Consciousness (an exchange of letters)

Springfield, New Jersey
June 12, 1972

Dear Prabhupāda,

I offer my humble obeisances.

I have been associating with the devotees of the New York temple. With the association of such fine, advanced devotees, I hope that I may make some advancement in Kṛṣṇa consciousness. My fiancee has started to come to the temple and is chanting a little. She knew nothing about Kṛṣṇa consciousness until I wrote her about it from India. Ātreya Ṛṣi has been kind enough to invite us to his home so that we may see an ideal householder life.

I went to Bombay the end of April for termination from the Peace Corps. I was fortunate enough to come down with a minor illness, so that I had to stay in Bombay for two weeks. I spent the time with the advanced and kind devotees at Juhu. Unfortunately you had left five days previously.

I understand so little, but I have faith in the process of Kṛṣṇa consciousness and hope to take to it more and more.

I look forward to Ātreya Ṛṣi's description of the temple in Los Angeles and hope that I may personally hear you in New York.

Thank you for the kindness you have shown to a very *undeserving* boy.

Sincerely,
Bob Cohen

A. C. Bhaktivedanta Swami
ISKCON Los Angeles
June 16, 1972

Bob Cohen
Springfield, New Jersey

My dear Bob,

Please accept my blessings. I thank you very much for your letter dated June 12, 1972. I have noted the sentiments expressed therein with great pleasure. I am very glad to hear that you are associating with us. I know that you are a very good boy, very intelligent, and your behavior is gentle, so I have all confidence that very quickly Kṛṣṇa will bestow all His blessings upon you, and you will feel yourself becoming perfectly happy in Kṛṣṇa consciousness. One makes his advancement in Kṛṣṇa consciousness by voluntarily giving up his attachment to material nature, or *māyā*. Such renunciation is called *tapasya*. But we are not very willing to perform austerities without good reason; therefore any man with a good scientific and philosophical mind, like your good self, must first appreciate what transcendental knowledge is. If you get knowledge, automatically *tapasya* will follow, and then you make your advancement in spiritual life. So to get knowledge is the first item for anyone who is hoping to find the perfection of his life. Therefore I advise you to read our books daily as far as possible and try to understand the subject matter from different angles of vision by discussing it frequently with the devotees at the New York temple. In this way you will gradually become convinced, and by your sincere attitude and devotional service you will make progress.

Yes, having some faith in me and in this Kṛṣṇa consciousness process is the first and only requirement for getting actual wisdom. If there is faith, understanding will follow. And as your understanding increases, so will your disgust with the spell of illusory energy. And when you voluntarily give up your entanglements in the material world, then the progress is assured.

I think we are just now typing up the tapes of those conversations we held in Māyāpur, and we shall be publishing them as a book. It will be called *Perfect Questions, Perfect Answers.* I shall send you a copy as soon as they are ready to distribute. Meanwhile, I shall be stopping in New York for two or three days on my way to London for the Ratha-yātrā Festival there. I am not yet certain when I shall be arriving in New York, but it will be some time in the early part of July. You may keep in regular contact with Bali Mardana regarding the arrival date, and I shall be very much engladdened to meet with you in New York once again. Again we shall discuss if you have any questions.

Hoping this will meet you in good health and a happy mood,

Your ever well-wisher,
A. C. Bhaktivedanta Swami

NINE

Deciding for the Future New York—July 4, 1972

BOB: I received your very kind letter.
ŚRĪLA PRABHUPĀDA: Oh.
BOB: About a week ago.
ŚRĪLA PRABHUPĀDA: Now, you are a very intelligent boy. You can try to understand this philosophy. It is very important. For sense gratification people are wasting so much energy. They are not aware of what is going to happen in the next life. There is a next life, but foolish people are ignorant. This life is preparation for the next life. That they do not know. The modern education and its universities are completely in darkness about this simple knowledge. We are changing bodies every moment—that is a medical fact. After leaving this body, we will have to accept another body. How are we going to accept that body? What kind of body? This can also be known. For example, if someone is being educated, one can understand that when he passes his examination, he is going to be an engineer or medical practitioner. Similarly, in this life, you can prepare yourself to become something in the next life.
BARBARA [Bob's wife]: Can we decide what we want to be next life?
ŚRĪLA PRABHUPĀDA: Yes, you can decide. We have decided that next life we are going to Kṛṣṇa. This is our decision—back home, back to Godhead. Suppose you want to become educated. After this decision that you are going

to be an engineer or you are going to be a medical practitioner, with that objective you prepare and educate yourself. Similarly, you can decide what you are going to do next life. But if you don't decide, then the material nature will decide.

BARBARA: Could I have been Kṛṣṇa conscious in my last life?

ŚRĪLA PRABHUPĀDA: It doesn't matter. But you can become. Take advantage of our Kṛṣṇa consciousness movement.

A DEVOTEE: She's asking if it was possible that in her last life she was a Kṛṣṇa devotee and has come back again.

ŚRĪLA PRABHUPĀDA: When one is perfectly Kṛṣṇa's devotee, he does not come back. But if there is a little deficiency, then there is a possibility of coming back. But even though there is a deficiency, he comes back to a nice family. *Śucīnāṁ śrīmatāṁ gehe yoga-bhraṣṭo 'bhijāyate.* ["The unsuccessful *yogī* takes birth in a religious or aristocratic family."] Human intelligence can decide for the future. That is human intelligence. The animal cannot decide. We have discriminatory power. If I do this, I will be benefited; if I do that, I will not be benefited. This is there in human life. So you have to use it properly. You should know what is our goal of life and decide in that way. That is human civilization....

BARBARA: Have you ever seen Kṛṣṇa?

ŚRĪLA PRABHUPĀDA: Yes.

BARBARA: You have?

ŚRĪLA PRABHUPĀDA: Daily. Every moment.

BARBARA: But not in the material body?

ŚRĪLA PRABHUPĀDA: He has no material body.

BARBARA: Well, in the temple here they have pictures of

Kṛṣṇa....

ŚRĪLA PRABHUPĀDA: That is not a material body. You are seeing materially because you have material eyes. Because you have material eyes, you cannot see the spiritual form. Therefore He kindly appears to be in a material body so that you can see. However, because He has kindly made Himself just fit for your seeing, that does not mean He has a material body. Suppose the President of the United States kindly comes to your house. That does not mean that his position and your position are the same. It is his kindness. Out of love, he may come to your house, but that does not mean he is on the same level as you. Similarly, because we cannot see Kṛṣṇa with our present eyes, Kṛṣṇa therefore appears before us as a painting, as made of stone, as made of wood. And Kṛṣṇa is not different from these paintings and wood because everything is Kṛṣṇa.

BARBARA: After we die, what happens to our spirit?

ŚRĪLA PRABHUPĀDA: You get another body.

BARBARA: Immediately?

ŚRĪLA PRABHUPĀDA: Yes. Just as when you change your apartment: you fix up your new apartment first; then you leave this one and go there.

BARBARA: So do we know what type of body we will get?

ŚRĪLA PRABHUPĀDA: Yes, provided you are qualified. Otherwise nature will arrange for it. Those who know—they know what is there. But for those who do not know, nature will arrange things. If you do not know, this means you have not prepared your life, so accidentally, at the time of death, your mentality will create another body, and nature will supply it.

BARBARA: And chanting—what does chanting do?

ŚRĪLA PRABHUPĀDA: That you can ask these boys [the

devotees]. They will explain.

BOB: If Kṛṣṇa controls everything, how does Kṛṣṇa control a nondevotee?

ŚRĪLA PRABHUPĀDA: By *māyā*. Just as the government controls everything. A kingdom is controlled by the king's departments.

BOB: And how does Kṛṣṇa control a devotee?

ŚRĪLA PRABHUPĀDA: Just as you control your beloved. For example, if you have a beloved child, you control him for his benefit. If he is going to touch fire, you will immediately tell him, "No, no, my dear child. Don't touch it." So a Kṛṣṇa conscious person, a devotee, is never misled, because Kṛṣṇa is always guiding him, whereas those who are not Kṛṣṇa conscious are in the charge of *māyā*, and *māyā* will do the needful, as you have seen.

BOB: Is it preset, when we're born, the time that we'll die?

ŚRĪLA PRABHUPĀDA: What?

BOB: Is the time that I'm going to die, and others are going to die, preset before we are born? When I'm born, do I have a certain given life span?

ŚRĪLA PRABHUPĀDA: Yes.

A DEVOTEE: And he cannot change that?

ŚRĪLA PRABHUPĀDA: No, he cannot change it, but Kṛṣṇa can change it.

DEVOTEE: If he commits suicide, is that also preset?

ŚRĪLA PRABHUPĀDA: Not preset. That you can do because you have a little independence. It is not natural to commit suicide; it is unnatural. So because we have independence, we can go from nature to "un-nature." A prisoner cannot go out of the prison house naturally, but somehow or other he arranges to jump over the wall and goes away. Then he becomes a criminal for further imprisonment. Naturally, the prisoner cannot go out of the prison house, but if somehow or other he manages to escape, that means he becomes again a criminal. He will be arrested again, and his term of imprisonment will be increased, or he will be punished more. So, naturally we cannot violate destiny. But if we do it, then we will suffer. But our destiny can be changed by Kṛṣṇa when we are Kṛṣṇa conscious. We do not do it, but Kṛṣṇa will do it. Kṛṣṇa says: *ahaṁ tvāṁ sarva-pāpebhyo mokṣayiṣyāmi:* "I shall give you protection." That change takes place for my protection.

There are two stages—nondevotee and devotee. The nondevotee is under the control of material nature, and the devotee is under the direct control of Kṛṣṇa. In the office of a big man, an executive of a big company, there are many employees, and they are controlled by different departmental superintendents. But although outside of home he controls indirectly, the same man at home is controlling his children directly. But he is always a controller. Similarly, God is the controller always. When one becomes a devotee, he is controlled by God; when he is a nondevotee, he is controlled by His agent, *māyā*. But he has to be controlled. For example, every citizen of America is controlled by the government. When he is all right, the civil department controls him; when he is not all right, the criminal department controls him. But he cannot say, "I am not controlled." That is not possible. Everyone is controlled. If somebody says, "I am not controlled," he is not sane; he is crazy. Everyone is controlled. So either you are controlled directly by God, or you are controlled by His agency, *māyā*. Being controlled by *māyā*, you spoil your life; you remain in material existence one birth after another, changing your bodies. But if you choose to be controlled by God, then after this body, you go back home, back to Godhead. Then your life is successful. You cannot exist without being controlled; that is not possible. That is intelligence. And that is stated in the *Bhagavad-gītā. Bahūnāṁ janmanām ante jñānavān māṁ prapadyate:* "After many births of traveling or speculation, one surrenders unto Me." *Vāsudevaḥ sarvam iti:* "Kṛṣṇa, You are everything. So I have come. Accept me. I am now fully surrendered unto You, and You control me. I am controlled. For so long I have been controlled by these rascals. There is no benefit. I have been controlled by my senses. So under the control of the senses I have served so-called family, society, country, nation—up to serving the dogs. But nothing has given me satisfaction. Therefore now I have good sense; I put myself under Your control. Instead of being controlled by dog, let me be controlled by God." This is Kṛṣṇa consciousness. Have you not seen how a man is controlled by a dog? In the street the dog stops, passes stool, and his master will stand and wait. Is it not? He is passing stool and urine, and the master is thinking, "I am master." But he is being controlled. That is *māyā*. He has become servant of the dog, but he is thinking, "I am master." So unless one is Kṛṣṇa conscious, one cannot understand. We can understand that this rascal is being controlled by his dog, but he is thinking that he is the master. We can understand. What do you think? Has he not become controlled by the dog?

BOB: That is so.

ŚRĪLA PRABHUPĀDA: But he is thinking, "I am the master of the dog." A family man is controlled by his wife, his children, by his servants, by everyone, but he is thinking,

"I am master." President Nixon is thinking that he is master of his country, but he is controlled. At once he can be dismissed by the public, his servants! And he will take a position, claiming, "I will give you very good service," and "I shall be a first-class servant." Therefore people vote, "All right, you become president." And he is advertising: "Reelect me! Reelect me!" That means he is a servant. But he is thinking, "I am master." That is the position. *Māyā*. One who is controlled by *māyā* is thinking himself master, but he is a servant. And a devotee never thinks to himself, "I am master," only "I am servant." That is the difference between *māyā* and reality. He at least knows: "I am never master. I am always a servant." When a servant is thinking, "I am master," that is called illusion. But when a servant thinks, "I am a servant," that is not illusion. That is *mukti,* liberation. Because he is not controlled by false thoughts. Try to think about this subject matter. A devotee is never controlled by false thoughts. He knows his position. *Svarūpena vyavasthitiḥ. Mukti,* liberation, means to be situated in one's own constitutional position. I am a servant. So if I know that I am a servant, that is my liberation. And if I think that I am master, that is bondage. This is the difference between conditioned life and liberated life.

So these Kṛṣṇa conscious devotees are always thinking that they are servants of Kṛṣṇa. Therefore they are all liberated. They do not endeavor for liberation. They are already liberated because they are situated in their constitutional position. They are not artificially thinking, "I am master." Otherwise, everyone is thinking, "I am master." That is illusion. You cannot be master in any state of your life; you must remain a servant. That is your position.

When one thinks artificially that he is master, that is his conditioned life. And when one voluntarily surrenders to the supreme master, that is his liberation. A devotee does not try for liberation separately. As soon as he surrenders to Kṛṣṇa or Kṛṣṇa's representative, he is liberated.

BOB: Prabhupāda, people that engage in religions, like these "Jesus freaks" and other people, claim that Jesus is guiding them. Can this be so?

ŚRĪLA PRABHUPĀDA: Yes, but they are not taking the guidance. Just like the Christians. Jesus is guiding them, "Thou shalt not kill," but they are killing. Where is the Jesus guidance? Simply saying, "I am guided by Jesus Christ"—will that do? "But I don't care for his words." Is that guidance? Nobody is being guided by Jesus Christ. Their claim is false. It is very hard to find a man who is actually being guided by Jesus Christ. Jesus Christ's guidance is available, but nobody is caring for him. They have taken Jesus Christ as contractor to take up their sins. That is their philosophy. They commit all kinds of sins, and poor Jesus Christ will be responsible. That is their religion. Therefore they say, "We have a very good religion. For all our sinful activities, Jesus Christ will die." So is that good religion? They have no sympathy for Jesus Christ. He died for our sins. Why should we commit sins again? Such a great life has been sacrificed for our sins, so we should be guided by Jesus Christ. But if you take it otherwise—"Ah, we shall go on committing all sins, and Jesus Christ will make a contract to nullify all my sins; I'll simply go to the church and confess and come back and again do all nonsense"—do you think that shows very good intelligence?

BOB: No.

ŚRĪLA PRABHUPĀDA: Actually, one who is guided by Jesus Christ will certainly get liberation. But it is very hard to find a man who is actually being guided by Jesus Christ.
BOB: What about the "Jesus freaks," the young people that have joined the Jesus movement? They read the Bible very often, and they try to—
ŚRĪLA PRABHUPĀDA: But violence is against the Bible's injunctions. How can they kill if they are following the Bible?
BOB: I asked one this, and he claimed that Jesus was also eating meat in the Bible.
ŚRĪLA PRABHUPĀDA: That's all right. He may eat anything. He is powerful. But he has ordered, "Thou shalt not kill. You must stop killing." He is powerful. He can eat the whole world. But you cannot compare to Jesus Christ. You cannot imitate Jesus Christ; you have to abide by his order. Then you are guided by Jesus Christ. That is actually obedience. That is explained in the *Bhāgavata*. One who is *īśvara*, who is empowered, can do anything, but we cannot imitate. We have to abide by his order: "What he says to me, that I will do." You cannot imitate. You say that Jesus Christ ate meat. Admitting that, you do not know in what condition he ate meat. He is himself eating meat, but he is advising others not to kill. Do you think that Jesus Christ was contradicting himself?
BOB: No.
ŚRĪLA PRABHUPĀDA: He cannot do that. That is real faith in him—that he cannot do that. So why has he eaten meat? He knows, but he has asked me not to kill. I have to follow. That is the real system. You are not Jesus Christ; you cannot imitate him. He has sacrificed his life for God. Can you do that? So why shall you imitate Jesus Christ?

You are imitating Jesus Christ by eating meat. Why not imitate Jesus Christ and sacrifice your life for spreading God consciousness? What do you think? Yes, when you preach you can say what you think. They are so-called Christians—but what are they doing for God? Just consider the sun. The sun is absorbing urine. Can you drink urine? If you want to imitate the sun—"Oh, here is the sun absorbing urine. Let me drink urine"—can you? Jesus Christ is powerful; he can do everything. But we cannot imitate; we have to simply abide by his order. That is real Christianity. We cannot imitate a powerful man. That is wrong. In our Vedic literature, there was a poison ocean, so people could not find out what to do with it. Then Lord Śiva said, "All right, I'll drink it." So he drank the whole poison ocean and kept it in his throat. Can you drink poison? Not the ocean—just one cup? So how can we imitate Lord Śiva? Lord Śiva never advised that we drink poison. So you have to abide by the advice, not imitate. These LSD and marijuana people say that Lord Śiva used to smoke *gañja*. But Lord Śiva drank the whole poisoned ocean. Can you do that? Lord Śiva's *instructions* should be taken. He says that the best worship is worship of Viṣṇu. *Viṣṇor ārādhanaṁ param*. When he was asked by Pārvatī what method of worship is best, then he said, "The best worship is worship of Lord Viṣṇu [Kṛṣṇa]." There are many demigods, but he recommended Viṣṇu worship as the best. And better than Viṣṇu worship is worship of a Vaiṣṇava. *Tadīyānām*—His servants, or those who are in relation to Him. For instance, we are worshiping this plant, *tulasī*. We are not worshiping all plants, but because this *tulasī* has a very intimate connection with Kṛṣṇa, Viṣṇu, we are therefore worshiping her. Similarly, if anything is

intimately related with Kṛṣṇa, worship of that thing is better than worship of Viṣṇu.
BOB: Why is that?
ŚRĪLA PRABHUPĀDA: Because Kṛṣṇa will be pleased. Suppose you have a dog and some friends come and pat your dog. [*Śrīla Prabhupāda makes big patting motions.*] You become pleased. You become pleased: "Oh, he is my good friend." You see how they think. We see this—some friend comes and says, "My, what a nice dog you have." [*Laughter.*] [*Some Indian guests enter the room.*]
ŚRĪLA PRABHUPĀDA: Please have some *prasāda.*
[*Śrīla Prabhupāda continues speaking with his guests, sometimes in English and sometimes Hindi. It is his last day in New York, and his plane to London is scheduled to leave in only a few hours, Bob has brought a car to drive Śrīla Prabhupāda to Kennedy Airport. The devotees are scurrying about, bringing luggage to the car, putting the manuscripts of Śrīla Prabhupāda's latest translating work in order, and making other last-minute arrangements.*]
ŚYĀMASUNDARA: Everything's ready, Śrīla Prabhupāda. The car is waiting for us.
ŚRĪLA PRABHUPĀDA: So? We can go now? All right. Hare Kṛṣṇa!

Concluding Words

On July 19, 1976, His Divine Grace Śrīla Prabhupāda accepted my wife and me as his disciples and initiated us with the names Bhakti-devī dāsī and Brahmatīrtha dāsa. As I reflect back on that day, I can see how fortunate I was to have met His Divine Grace and my Godbrothers in the Hare Kṛṣṇa movement.

When I was handed my beads at initiation, I promised to follow the regulative principles and to chant God's names daily. Four years previously, Śrīla Prabhupāda had advised me to follow these principles, and within six months, he said, I could be like the other devotees; all unnecessary things (*anarthas*), such as mundane movies and restaurants, would cease to attract me. "The whole human life is meant for purification," he said. I was interested in being purified, even though I did not really know what purification meant. I had gone to India with the Peace Corps hoping to find a higher level of consciousness. I could not believe that satisfying the senses was the all in all, yet I myself was bound by the senses. Later I could understand that *yoga* means becoming free from the dictation of the senses.

Upon returning to America, I started graduate school in geology, got married, and became somewhat entangled in domestic responsibilities, but I would very often think of my conversations with Śrīla Prabhupāda, and of his instructions. One of his primary instructions was simply to associate with the devotees, and this I gladly did. Devotees are different: by understanding that loving service to the Supreme Lord is the goal of life, they avoid getting caught up in the petty affairs of sense gratification and false ego. Visiting the temple was most refreshing. Gradually, my wife and I became friends with many devotees and wanted somehow to do some service for the movement. I sponsored a *bhakti-yoga* club at the university, and our apartment served as a way station for traveling parties of devotees.

As we followed Śrīla Prabhupāda's instructions, even our eating became purified. In India I had told Śrīla Prabhupāda that I could not offer my food as the devotees do because I did not understand that Kṛṣṇa is God. So he told me simply to thank God for my food before eating. This we did, and finally our devotion matured, and we started actually offering our food to the Supreme Lord. What a wonderful feeling, to be cooking for the Supreme Lord! This actually freed us from the control of the tongue.

Finally, we were ready to become involved fully in temple life. By Kṛṣṇa's grace, I obtained a job near a temple in Texas and began to take part in all the temple programs. In this way, all the *anarthas* disappeared, just as Śrīla Prabhupāda had predicted. It was like having a burden lifted from our shoulders. We were no longer servants of our senses, but servants of God and His devotees. The value of Śrīla Prabhupāda's instructions had become clear. A human being is not meant to labor like an ass and enjoy like a dog. Purification means coming to a higher level of consciousness.

Even though I have been initiated, I still admire my Godbrothers' spiritual awareness and wish to advance. Actually, initiation is the beginning.

Brahmatīrtha dāsa Adhikārī
(Bob Cohen)

Houston, Texas
October 16, 1976

His Divine Grace A.C. Bhaktivedanta Swami Prabhupāda

His Divine Grace A.C. Bhaktivedanta Swami Prabhupāda appeared in this world in 1896 in Calcutta, India. He first met his spiritual master, Śrīla Bhaktisiddhānta Sarasvāti Gosvāmi, in Calcutta in 1922. Bhaktsiddhānta Sarasvatī, a prominent devotional scholar and the founder of sixty-four Gauḍīya Maṭhas (Vedic institutes), liked this educated young man and convinced him to dedicate his life to teaching Vedic knowledge. Śrīla Prabhupāda became his student, and eleven years later (1933) at Allahabad he became his formally initiated disciple

At their first meeting, in 1922, Śrīla Bhaktsiddhānta Sarasvatī Ṭhākura requested Śrīla Prabhupāda to broadcast Vedic knowledge through the English language. In the years that followed, Śrīla Prabhupāda wrote a commentary on the *Bhagavad-gītā,* assisted the Gauḍīya Maṭha in its work and, in 1944, without assistance, started an English fortnightly magazine, edited it, typed the manuscripts and checked the galley proofs. He even distributed the individual copies freely and struggled to maintain the publication. Once begun, the magazine never stopped; it is now being continued by his disciples in the West.

Recognizing Śrīla Prabhupāda's philosophical learning and devotion, the Gauḍīya Vaiṣṇava Society honored him in 1947 with the title "Bhaktivedanta." In 1950, at the age of fifty-four, Śrīla Prabhupāda retired from married life, and four years later he adopted the *vānaprastha* (retired) order to devote more time to his studies and writing. Śrīla Prabhupāda traveled to the holy city of Vṛndāvana, where he lived in very humble circumstances in the historic medieval temple of Rādhā-Dāmodara. There he engaged for several years in deep study and writing. He accepted the renounced order of life (*sannyāsa*) in 1959. At Rādhā-Dāmodara, Śrīla Prabhupāda began work on his life's masterpiece: a multivolume translation and commentary on the eighteen-thousand-verse *Śrīmad-Bhāgavatam* (*Bhāgavata Purāṇa*). He also wrote *Easy Journey to Other Planets.*

After publishing three volumes of *Bhāgavatam* Śrīla Prabhupāda came to the United States, in 1965, to fulfill the mission of his spiritual master. Since that time, His Divine Grace has written over forty volumes of authoritative translations, commentaries and summary studies of the philosophical and religious classics of India.

In 1965, when he first arrived by freighter in New York City, Śrīla Prabhupāda was practically penniless. It was after almost a year of great difficulty that he established the International Society for Krishna Consciousness in July of 1966. Under his careful guidance, the society has grown within a decade to a worldwide confederation of almost one hundred *āśramas,* schools, temples, institutes and farm communities..

In 1968, Śrīla Prabhupāda created New Vṛndāvana, an experimental Vedic community in the hills of West Virginia. Inspired by the success of New Vṛndāvana, now a thriving farm community of more than one thousand acres, his students have since founded several similar communities in the United States and abroad.

In 1972, His Divine Grace introduced the Vedic system of primary and secondary education in the West by founding the Gurukula school in Dallas, Texas. The school began with three children in 1972, and by the beginning of 1975 the enrolment had grown to one hundred fifty.

Śrīla Prabhupāda has also inspired the construction of a large international center at Śrīdhāma Māyāpur in West Bengal, India, which is also the site for a planned institute of Vedic studies. A similar project is the magnificent Kṛṣṇa Balarāma Temple and International Guest House in Vṛndāvana, India. These are centers where Westerners can live to gain firsthand experience of Vedic culture.

Śrīla Prabhupāda's most significant contribution, however, is his books. Highly respected by the academic community for their authoritativeness, depth and clarity, they are used as standard textbooks in numerous college courses. His writings have been translated into eleven languages. The Bhaktivedanta Book Trust, established in 1972 , exclusively to publish the works of His Divine Grace, has thus become the world's largest publisher of books in the field of Indian religion and philosophy. Its latest project is the publishing of Śrīla Prabhupāda's most recent work: a seventeen-volume translation and commentary—compiled by Śrīla Prabhupāda in only eighteen months—on the Bengali religious classic *Śrī Caitanya-caritāmṛta.*

In the past ten years, in spite of his advanced age, Śrīla Prabhupāda has circled the globe twelve times on lecture tours that have taken him to six continents. In spite of such a vigorous schedule, Śrīla Prabhupāda continues to write prolifically. His writings constitute a veritable library of Vedic philosophy, religion, literature and culture.

Glossary

Ācārya—a spiritual master who teaches by example.
Ārati—a ceremony for greeting the Lord with offerings of food, lamps, fans, flowers and incense.
Arcanā—the devotional practice of Deity worship.
Āśrama—a spiritual order of life.
Asuras—atheistic demons.
Avatāra—a descent of the Supreme Lord.

Bhagavad-gītā—the basic directions for spiritual life spoken by the Lord Himself.
Bhakta—a devotee.
Bhakti-yoga—linking with the Supreme Lord in ecstatic devotional service.
Brahmacarya—celibate student life; the first order of Vedic spiritual life.
Brahman—the Absolute Truth; especially, the impersonal Aspect of the Absolute.
Brāhmaṇa—a person in the mode of goodness; first Vedic social order.

Dharma—eternal occupational duty; religious principles.

Ekādaśī—a special fast day for increased remembrance of Kṛṣṇa, which comes on the eleventh day of both the waxing and waning moon.

Goloka (Kṛṣṇaloka)—the highest spiritual planet, con-

taining Kṛṣṇa's personal abodes, Dvārakā, Mathurā and Vṛndāvana.
Gopis—Kṛṣṇa's cowherd girl friends who are His most confidential servitors.
Gṛhastha—regulated household life; the second order of Vedic spiritual life.
Guru—a spiritual master or superior person.

Hare Kṛṣṇa *mantra*—See: *Mahā-mantra*.

Jiva-tattva—the living entities, who are small parts of the Lord.

Kali-yuga (Age of Kali)—the present age, which is characterized by quarrel. It is last in the cycle of four, and began five thousand years ago.
Karatālas—hand cymbals used in *kīrtana*.
Karma—fruitive action, for which there is always reaction, good or bad.
Karmī—one who is satisfied with working hard for flickering sense gratification.
Kirtana—chanting the glories of the Supreme Lord.
Kṛṣṇaloka—See: Goloka.
Kṣatriyas—a warrior or administrator; the second Vedic social order.

Mahā-mantra—the great chanting for deliverance: Hare Kṛṣṇa, Hare Kṛṣṇa, Kṛṣṇa Kṛṣṇa, Hare Hare/ Hare Rāma, Hare Rāma, Rāma Rāma, Hare Hare.
Mantra—a sound vibration that can deliver the mind from illusion.
Mathurā—Lord Kṛṣṇa's abode, surrounding Vṛndāvana,

where He took birth and later returned to after performing His Vrndāvana pastimes.
Māyā—(*mā*—not; *yā*—this), illusion; forgetfulness of one's relationship with Kṛṣṇa.
Māyāvādīs—impersonal philosophers who say that the Lord cannot have a transcendental body.
Mṛdaṅga—a clay drum used for congregational chanting.

Paramparā—the chain of spiritual masters in disciplic succession.
Prasāda—food spiritualized by being offered to the Lord.

Sac-cid-ānanda-vigraha—the Lord's transcendental form, which is eternal, full of knowledge and bliss.
Saṅkīrtana—public chanting of the names of God, the approved *yoga* process for this age.
Sannyāsa—renounced life; the fourth order of Vedic spiritual life.
Śravaṇaṁ kīrtanaṁ viṣṇoḥ—the devotional process of hearing and chanting about Lord Viṣṇu.
Śāstras—revealed scriptures.
Śūdra—a laborer; the fourth of the Vedic social orders.
Svāmī—one who controls his mind and senses; title of one in the renounced order of life.

Tapasya—austerity; accepting some voluntary inconvenience for a higher purpose.
Tilaka—auspicious clay marks that sanctify a devotee's body as a temple of the Lord.

Vaikuṇṭha—the spiritual world, where there is no anxiety.
Vaiṣṇava—a devotee of Lord Viṣṇu, or Kṛṣṇa.

Vaiśyas—farmers and merchants; the third Vedic social order.

Vānaprastha—one who has retired from family life; the third order of Vedic spiritual life.

Varṇāśrama—the Vedic social system of four social and four spiritual orders.

Vedas—the original revealed scriptures, first spoken by the Lord Himself.

Viṣṇu, Lord—Kṛṣṇa's first expansion for the creation and maintenance of the material universes.

Vṛndāvana—Kṛṣṇa's personal abode, where He fully manifests His quality of sweetness.

Vyāsadeva—Kṛṣṇa's incarnation, at the end of Dvāpara-yuga, for compiling the Vedas.

Yajña—sacrifice, work done for the satisfaction of Lord Viṣṇu.

Yogī—a transcendentalist who, in one way or another, is striving for union with the Supreme.

Yuga—ages in the life of a universe, occurring in a repeated cycle of four.